Albert Morlan

A Hoosier in Honduras

Albert Morlan

A Hoosier in Honduras

ISBN/EAN: 9783743337169

Manufactured in Europe, USA, Canada, Australia, Japa

Cover: Foto ©ninafisch / pixelio.de

Manufactured and distributed by brebook publishing software (www.brebook.com)

Albert Morlan

A Hoosier in Honduras

A Hoosier In Honduras,

By Albert Morlan.

ILLUSTRATED.

El Dorado Publishing Company,
Indianapolis, Ind.

CONTENTS.

CHAPTER I.
How it came to pass and other matters pertaining to the start. Belize.—Inhabitants and history........................ 5

CHAPTER II.
At the "American Hotel."—A Carib village, historical sketch of this strange people—A funeral—Sail on the Rio Dulce 27

CHAPTER III.
Something about bananas—Arrive at Puerto Cortez—Touch of the chills—Model hotel.................................. 49

CHAPTER IV.
A cruise along the north coast of Honduras—Visit Truxillo—Landing—Study a waterspout—Walker the filibuster—Spanish cruelty and English perfidy............................ 67

CHAPTER V.
Visit the Bay Islands, Bonacca, Ruatan, Utilla—Night of storm back at the port.................................... 85

CHAPTER VI.
Great trans-continental railroad—Flying trip over the same—Town of San Pedro—Small earthquake—Waiting............. 99

CHAPTER VII.
Services of Moses and Aaron secured—Final arrangements for the overland trip—The start—Among the mountains—Santa Cruze and its mines—Primitive villages—Beautiful scenery, 111

CHAPTER VIII.
A pleasant surprise—Colines and a wedding—Drink the bride's health and loose our own—Beautiful days on the road—Santa Barbara—Home of the President—Loss of Moses and Aaron.. 127

CHAPTER IX.
From Santa Barbara to the Capitol, with some digressions....... 143

CHAPTER X.
Tegucigalpa—Interview with the President—Off for the coast—Arrive at Amapala............................. 165

CHAPTER XI.
City of Leon—An honest cabman—Momotombo—Storm on Lake Managua—Arrive at the Capitol—Its industries............. 181

CHAPTER XII.
City of Grenada—Hotel de Los Leons.......................... 197

Preface.

It was the writers intention to impose this work on the public without the formality of a preface. It seemed bad enough as it was, but certain critical friends declared it would never do, "You must offer some excuse," they insisted, "for writing a book at all, the people have not asked for it and it is no more than right they should have an explanation of the motive that prompted so reckless an undertaking."

I, therefore, began looking over a lot of books, ancient and modern, hoping to find something to copy and save any further trouble, but when I saw that most writers devoted the space under this heading to giving credit to certain other writers whose works they had filched to produce their own, I said, "I'll never do it." The reader may pick out the stolen passages himself, and if his conscience is too sensitive to allow him to retain them—why, he can return them to their respective owners. I had enough trouble to steal them, and besides I can't remember now just where they belong, so if the dear reader can construe this into an apology, and feels any better satisfied thereby, the writer is very glad indeed, and feels more than paid for the exertion it has cost.

As for a motive, I had absolutely none, beyond the sordid one, of selling you a copy, which having accomplished, I wish to thank you personally for your contribution and beg to remain,

                              Yours very truly,

Indianapolis, Ind.   THE AUTHOR.

ON THE RIO DULCE—GAUTEMALA.

A Hoosier in Honduras.

CHAPTER I.

HOW IT CAME TO PASS AND OTHER MATTERS PERTAINING TO THE START—BELIZE: INHABITANTS AND HISTORY.

One bleak winter day the writer conceived the brilliant idea of escaping cold blasts and gas bills by taking an excursion tropicward, while pondering on the subject the postman appeared with a letter, which upon examination proved an invitation to join a trading expedition to the interior of Honduras, with side trips into Gautemala and Nicaragua, to say nothing of a coast wise pilgrimage which was also to include the Bay Islands. Some passages in this brief communication fired the immagination, and the youthful longing to visit the scenes of romantic adventure recorded by the followers of Columbus, Cortez, Balboa and other equally daring albeit, reckless characters, was at once revived. Other sentences bordered on the sentimental, for the letter was from an old friend, and if he occasionally approached the poetical form of expression he was certainly to be excused. Even the practical business man, will sometimes forget himself, so in this instance memories of childish exploits and asperations were vividly recalled.

"Together we will sail the 'sunny summer seas' that we used to dream about; climb gold veined mountains, explore mahogany forests, examine volcanoes, study earthquakes"—but enough—the concluding lines seemed to settle the matter" I await your letter of acceptance," said he, "and have quite decided not to listen to any excuses—come."

Outside the air was thick with falling snow, and huge icicles hung from the eaves. The bare branches of an old cherry tree lashed the side of the house in remembrance of some old grudge, maybe—or perhaps it was simply because the furious blast aroused a spirit of animosity which was in a measure appeased by thrashing the only object within reach.

A few of the nearest houses could be seen, and these but dimly through the ever increasing storm. The street with its long rows of telephone poles and trolley supports was swallowed up in a strange white gloom. From time to time, the dim outline of some venturesome pedestrian would appear for an instant before the window, struggling bravely with the tempest, the next moment they were swept from view. The heavy trucks and express wagons that usually filled the air with their din, now stole by as silent as a funeral train, the drivers looking like sheeted ghosts who had somehow escaped the grip of death and returned to their duty, silent and sad, and white as the street below.

Only the voice of the wind was heard as it rattled the windows and shook the doors, now shrieking with rage, now moaning in despair to find every opening stoutly locked against it—such was the day when the shivering carrier, half blinded by the storm, brought the brief message referred to.

According to the terms of the invitation, there seemed but one thing to do,—therefore a letter of acceptance was penned and posted.—

In about two weeks came the reply. He now wrote more fully, even enclosing a catalogue of articles necessary to the comfort of travelers in a tropical wilderness, among which were "slickers" to protect us from the storms on the mountains, saddles, blankets, leggings, spurs, hammocks, a chest of medicine, a small selection of books, a bundle of newspapers, a great variety of canned goods, with a lot of "cordials" put up in large long-necked bottles, these were only to be used in cases of emergency,—of course. The list also included a stock of rubber goods to protect us from dampness when sailing those "Sunny Summer Seas" which he now admitted became quite rough at times when teased by the vagrant winds that loaf around in those latitudes.

I learned later that my correspondent was a very careful, conservative writer, and his intimations regarding the weather were in no wise exaggerated, in fact he might have drawn a much more vivid picture of those laughing waves and rollicking winds and still left a wide margin for my imagination to sketch in, for I had no conception of the force of the tornadoes, cyclones and hurricanes that occasionally sweep across the otherwise calm surface of the Carribean Sea.

This letter was followed by another, a few days later with fuller information, and an additional list of "necessaries" which included such trifles as thread, needles, pins, buttons, cork-screws, knives, forks, cups and a hundred other articles that are called for every day in civilized life, but which we are so accustomed to that we are quite unconscious of their usefulness—however, a couple of weeks busy preparation saw the work completed, and, one cold, clear morning I took the train amid huge drifts of snow. Forty hours latter found us walking between walls of roses, in the city of New Orleans, where we spent a few days looking over this, the quainest city in the United States. We explored the French quarter with its famous market, the ancient cathedral, Jackson's Park, the old slave market, the warfs, the large, elegant stores, which line Canal Street, from which the canal has disappeared and its place taken by a street railway, over whose tracks small, uncomfortable cars are drawn by unwilling mules, whose eccentric dispositions keep the driver in a state of uncertain expectancy that has driven some to suicide and others to drink. After having visited the Spanish fort, the cemetaries and the famous "shell roads," which by the way are sadly out of repair, we sought the office of the Machecka Bros., 129 Decatur street and purchased tickets for Belize and shortly took possession of our quarters on board the "Break-water," Captain C. W. Clark commanding; a little over three days—or to be more accurate, a little less than four days sailing brought us within sight of the pretty little city of Belize, which is the capital of British Honduras, the largest and most important port on the eastern coast of Central America. The approach to this place is interesting from the fact that it was for many years the rendezvous of an organized band of pirates, who practically ruled the Western Seas for a generation or so in the seventeenth century. Each wooded island and rocky "spit" has its legends of buried treasures, which, however, is so carefully guarded by the Spirits of the departed, or was so cleverly hidden, that no one has ever been able to locate a single "cache," although we read almost every week of wonderful "finds" of this character, investigation invariably proved the story to be, either a newspaper hoax cut out of the whole cloth, or the gradual accumulation of gossip, growing out of some insignificant circumstance, such as the discovery of a fragment of ancient crockery or other ship's stores which had been

HON. A. E. MORLAN, U. S. CONSUL, PORT OF BELIEZ.

U. S. CONSULATE.

thrown on shore after some wreck. I doubt if there is a single authentic case on record where treasure in any appreciable quantity has been found—however, each year brings fresh victims from all parts of the world, every one of whom feel confident they have the "key" to these mysterious deposits of wealth, and after spending all the money they possess, return to their respective homes, sadder and poorer, possibly wiser. They come from everywhere armed with "divining rods," "witches wands," "magnetic indicators," and a hundred other devices invented by the ingenious Yankee, to meet the demands of these fortune seeking hordes, which seem to increase rather than diminish, with the passing years. Indeed, so great has been the rush of treasure hunters, during the last decade, the government has taken advantage of the craze and now issues a regular licence or "privilege" which has proved quite a source of revenue. The shrewd official who drew up this document, inserted a clause providing that a certain proportion of the wealth recovered shall become the property of the crown, or words to that effect, thus conveying the impression that the government indorses the absurd tales concerning the hidden spoils of the ancient but indiscreet buccaneer.

The fact is, the old pirates of the seventeeth century were not such fools as to bury their hard-earned wealth where they could not find it when wanted, and there is probably very little foundation for the extravagant yarns that have been handed down from generation to generation, acquiring new and startling features from time to time at the hands of those who feed their imagination on these grotesque and improbable traditions. Many practical jokes have been perpetrated on the credulous cranks who pass their lives dreaming of the wealth that might have been honestly acquired, perhaps, by the systematic saving of the depised penny.

As has been stated, many practical jokes are played on these unsuspecting dreamers, but so eager and blind are they, as a rule, that the most transparent counterfeit passes without question. Most of these fairy tales have their origin in the fertile brain of some Jack Tar of whose ingenuity and industry, in the matter of romancing, all the world knows. Here is a specimen:

Jim L———, second mate of the good ship B———, who had been born on the water and who had, to use his own expression, never been out of his "mother's lap" in all the fifty-five years of his eventful life, was one of those whose chief delight consisted in catering to the abnormal appetites of these seekers after lost treasures, and his leisure hours were mainly devoted to the construction of charts, showing the exact location of the hidden wealth, entering into all the details with a minuteness that left the possessor no room to doubt his ability to go right to the spot and dig it up. In some of these, a very careful invoice of the money and valuables was given showing precisely where each lot was located—all by characters or ciphers, no words being used.

These charts would sometimes turn up at an auction in London, or Paris, or perhaps would be discovered in the chest of a dead seaman, or some junk shop, or, in some instances, they were cast adrift to be picked up on the shores of one of the numerous cays in the neighborhood, but wherever they appeared they aroused the enthusiasm of the idle dreamers, and were welcomed by the world at large, for to tell the truth, there are few so practical that stories of hidden millions will not for a moment at least find interest in the tale, no matter how improbable it may be. The following cut is a fac-simile of one of these bogus charts, and shows on what dubious foundations these collosal structures of the imagination often rest, and on what flimsy pretexts, men, apparently sane, in other matters, will leave home and business, often investing large sums in the venture and not infrequently completing the sacrifice with their lives, as did a certain Mr. Horn whose excursions in this romantic field is the excuse for this article with its illustration, and if by its publication some poor dupe is saved the sad experience that is sure to follow adventures of this character, the writer will feel amply rewarded.

This ingenious work was executed with great care on a piece of parchment which had been previously prepared by staining to give it the appearance of age. The figures were drawn with a camel hair pencil, the medium used was an indelible ink of light brown color which penetrated the material and could not be erased:

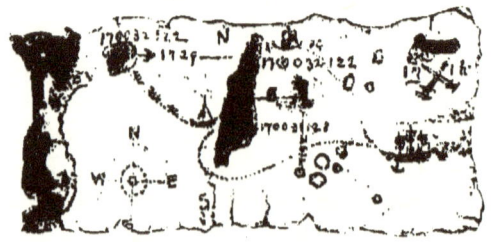

THE DELUSIVE CHART.

It was some such document that had fallen into the hands of the Mr. Horn aboved referred to, on the head of which he had embarked in the hazardous enterprise which proved so disastrous. The amount of treasure accounted for by the "key", in his possession, was, he declared, about $1,400,000 and he confidently expected to return to the states with this amount in a few weeks at the farthest. How he succeeded will be told in another chapter.

To those who care to investigate the subject, the following extract from a recent writer on "Treasure Trove," may prove interesting. "According to the laws of England the finder of coin, gold and silver plate or bullion, providing the same be *hidden in the earth*, is not entitled to the treasure but must give notice to the crown, to whom it belongs. If, however, the treasure is *not hidden in and covered up* by the earth, it becomes the property of the finder. The various colonies, however, have laws of their own, modified to suit the conditions, for instance, in India the finder holds the entire amount discovered, providing no owner can be found. In case the rightful owner appears the finder is entitled to *three-fourths* of the amount while the real owner must be satisfied with one-fourth only. However, the government reserves the right to purchase by the payment of *one-fifth more* than the value of the material."

It was Sunday morning bright, calm, beautiful. The view from the deck, as we picked our way slowly and cautiously among the numerous cays and low green islands, was enchanting. In the far distance the white buildings of the city peeped timidly out from between long rows of royal palms, with here and there a clump of cocanut trees, easily distinguishable even at this distance by their long twisted trunks surmounted by a tuft of foiliage that looked almost black when contrasted with the brighter greens of the other vegetation. The immediate foreground was enlivened by a variety of sailing craft, with here and there an English Merchantman lying at anchor rocking gently with the swell of the sea. Occasionally a warning flag, or a bright red buoy, told of hidden rocks.

At last we found ourselves fairly within the harbor where we anchored perhaps a half mile from shore. Here we were met by the officials of the Custom House who carefully went through our luggage, but finding nothing of a dangerous nature we were permitted to land. As we stepped ashore we were met by a young man representing Mr. Christo Hempsted, who with his family was enjoying a weeks outing at one of the numerous resorts within a few hours sail of the city. Through his representative, he begged us to take possession of his house during his absence, which we with characteristic freedom proceeded to do. Within a few minutes after landing we found ourselves delightfully situated in the comfortable and roomy dwelling of our friend and fellow countryman, for Mr. Hemsted although a resident of Belize for more than twenty years, still retains his American citizenship, and withall is one of the best and biggest hearted men in Central America. Here we remained for several days.

Meanwhile we accepted a pressing invitation from Mrs. Capt. Biddle, to be present regularly at her table, an invitation that was accepted with cheerful alacrity, and which proved one of the pleasantest features of our visit, and it is with genuine pleasure that the writer hereby expresses his gratitude to this estimable lady for the many favors shown him during his stay in Belize.

The history of the colonly of British Honduras is interesting, from the fact that it is the only English dependency in Central America. The following facts concerning its discovery and subsequent settlement, are taken from the "British Honduras Almanac," a veritable encyclopedia of information, and which has been issued annually for more than fifty years and is lovingly referred to by Mr. John L. Stevens in his "Incidents of Travel in Yucatan," etc. A. D. 1839.

"This colony is deserving of interest both on account of the romance of its past history and the promise of the importance and commercial success which it at present holds out. Situated as it is between 18 degrees 29 min. 5 sec. and 15 degrees 23 min. 55 sec. North Latitude and between 9 degrees 9 min. 22 sec. and 88 degrees 10 min. West Longitude, it contains some of the richest and most fertile lands on the face of the globe. To it Europe has to look for the greater part of its supplies of mahogany and logwood, the exportation of which is alone sufficient to render it a wealthy and thriving colony and in addition to the large interests involved in the supply of these and other valuable woods, there now seems every probability of its becoming of equal importance as a center for the exports for the various fruits which grow so abundantly on the seward slopes of Yucatan.

The climate, though damp and hot, is singularly healthy. Yellow fever and cholera are but rare visitors. Ague and malaria though somewhat more frequent, are by no means as prevalent as might be expected. To the north and south its boundaries are respectively the frontiers of Yucatan and Guatemala, while to the east it is bounded by the Bay of Honduras and to the west by a line laid down by the convention with Guatemala in 1859, extending from the rapids of Gracios A Dios on the river Sarstoon, to Garbutt's Falls on the Belize river and thence due north to the Mexican Frontier. The coast was discovered by Columbus in 1502 when looking for a passage to the China Seas and the interior is the scene, in part at least, of the famous and disastrous march of Cortez. The greatest length and breadth of the colony are respectively 174 and 68 statute miles, containing with the adjacent cays an area of about 7,562 square miles. The settlement was originally called Belize, the name now applied to the capitol only. It is supposed by some that it was originally settled by Buccaniers, who were attracted to the coast by the shelter and safety afforded to them by the extreme difficulty of navigation among the surrounding cays and who were induced to remain on the dispersion of their main forces with the hope of gaining wealth in a more legitimate manner by cutting the woods of the country, and they were wise in their day, for who, but a lunatic would risk life and limb in the somewhat doubtful business of plundering an occasional ship when they could, by a few hours labor with a good axe, bring down a fortune of $2,500 to $3,000, for in the middle of the seventeenth century, logwood sold readily for $100 per ton, which has gradually fallen until at the present writing the price is only about $6.

In 1671 Sir Thomas Lynch, Govenor of Jamaica, reported to the King that "it increased his Majesty's custom and the national commerce more than any of his Majesty's colonies," showing that Belize was a flourishing and wealthy settlement more than 200 years ago. From that time up to 1798 the territory was the cause of much bitter contention between England and Spain, which occasionally resulted in bloody conflicts. In 1786 England agreed to relinquish the Mosquito Shore in exchange for the privilege of cutting mahogany and logwood. By this treaty, England promised to abstain from erecting fortifications or other defensive works, thereby admitting the colony was, in name at least, under

Spanish protection." This was what a Yankee would term a good trade. The Mosquito Shore was a howling wilderness noted only for its scorpions, centipedes and the swarms of those interesting little insects from which it takes its name, while Belize enjoyed a remarkably salubrious climate for this latitude, besides abounding in those woods that had already proved more profitable than mines of gold or silver. Of course, the Spaniards soon discovered how they had been outwitted and determined to re-possess the valuable claim by force of arms, and to that end assembled a fleet of fifteen vessels with which, on September 10, 1798, they began an attack on the Harbor of Belize and after two days severe fighting were totally defeated in the memorable "Battle of St. Georges' Caye," which event has been celebrated by Mr. Christo Hempstead, the local poet, in the following stiring lines:

ST. GEORGES' CAYE.

'Twas a dark, sultry and warm summers' night,
When St. Geoeges' Caye people saw a wonderful sight,
A bungay full of Spaniards all armed for a fray,
Came sailing from windward, o'er Honduras Bay.

CHORUS.

Sing to rol ri urol—ri urol ri—a
And they drove all those Spaniards so far, far away.
Sing tu rol ri urol—ri urol urol ri—a
And they made them all scamper from St. Georges' "K."

The battle was fierce, and the battle was strong,
The *"Pork and Dough-Boys"* sticks, were both sharp and long,
And each hardy "Bayman" grasped one in his hand,
Saying we'll "chook" (spear) all those Spaniards the moment they land.

REPEAT CHORUS.

They "chooked" them, and speared them and drove them like fleas,
Right into salt water way up to their knees,
Some got to their bungays and poled quick away,
Saying—"*Vamonos Compadre*" from St Georges' "K."

REPEAT CHORUS.

The battle now over, a victory hard brought,
Each gallant old "Bayman" like the devil had fought,
But thus gained their freedom by the sweat of their brow,
And that was the end of St. Georges' "K" row.

REPEAT CHORUS.

The bungay got lost is the general belief,
Way out on the "Spit," on a small bit of reef,

Naught was ever seen of her keelson or keel,
And "nary" a spaniard or General O'Neal.*

REPEAT CHORUS.

Tune: Wilkins and his Dianah.

* " General O'Neal was supposed to be a renegade, who deserted from the "Baymen" and went over to the Spaniards.

Thus it was that the settlement became English by right of conquest as well as by convention."

The city of Belize is probably the most cosmopolitan in character of any place in the world of its size. Its population of eight or ten thousand includes citizens of England, France, Spain, Germany, Italy, Africa, China, South America, Mexico, the United States and Canada, not to mention the native Indians, Creoles, cock-roaches, fleas, land crabs, ants, scorpions, sandflies, mosquitoes, and turkey buzzards, locally known as "John Crows."

This is a land of social and political equality and no discrimination is made in favor of any class except in the cases of the buzzard and roach. The former is protected by a special act of the legislature making the shooting of one of these birds punishable by a fine of $25.00 for each offense. Although the price seemed quite reasonable, we refrained from killing any of them simply because it was not the style, besides one hates to see a man going around making a display of his wealth.

The case of the cock-roach is different. He is protected by the stronger law of public opinion, consequently he assumes a degree of audacity unparalleled in any other country. Among the privileges accorded his lordship, the most notable is that of bathing in the water pitcher at all hours, but do not loose your temper, it is his right. Lift him out gently, place in a comfortable position on a chair, bowing low, you will beg his pardon for interrupting his aquatic performance. You may now take a drink, providing you still have the desire. O, don't think to escape his tyranny by drinking wine or beer for his authority extends over the whole territory and must be recognized alike by rich and poor. These are not the modest little fellows that are occasionally seen in the northern groceries glancing timidly around and vanishing like smoke at the slightest alarm, but great lordly loafers grown proud and arrogant through untold generations of supremacy. He is everywhere, on the table, in the bookcase, in the pantry, in the parlor, upstairs and down, in the bed and under it. When you wake from clammy dreams you will find him mounted on the high post at the foot of your couch, looking down on you with lofty disdain, as he muses on the mutibility of man and his works. When he moves, he does so with "kingly leisure and courtly grace." He is "monarch of all he surveys," and he traverses his domain in imperial state.

Belize is the negro's paradise. Here he enjoys every privilege that is accorded his white brother, and some besides, I am told.

In the shops you are met by smiling, black clerks; on the street you are jostled by a good-natured black throng. The police are black, likewise the mail-carriers and postal clerks.

The police force, by the way, is said to be very efficient, being composed of the "pick" of the province. They are tall, well proportioned, finely uniformed, and bear themselves as proudly as Roman soldiers.

CUSTOM HOUSE.

The government is very indulgent to its prisoners, allowing them to take a stroll about town every morning, from 8 to 12 o'clock, and for exercise they are permitted to break stone or make any necessary improvements on the streets, for which they are very grateful, no doubt.

I met a squad one morning starting out for their daily walk, and noticed with pleasure the tender-hearted policy that sent a couple of officers along with the gang to see that they did not get hurt or lost in their rambles. To enable the officers to properly protect their wards they were armed with double-barrelled, breech-loading shot guns.

Each convict had his name and number conspicuously lettered in bright red on the back of his shirt, which added not a little to their picturesque appearance.

The houses are all frame, with one or two exceptions, and those of the better class, usually being three stories in height with balconies and wide verandas, over which are trained vines and climbing roses. The buildings are nearly all painted white with green blinds and the effect is charming. Flowers in endless variety flourish throughout the year, filling the air with their fragrance, among these, the oleander is one of the most conspicuous, the tree attaining here its greatest perfection, often reaching a hight of twelve feet, its pink and white blossoms, contrasting beautifully with the dark green foliage of the mango trees, which are planted extensively for shade as well as fruit.

The streets, which stretch away in every direction, were laid out without regard to regularity. They cross each other at every possible angle, and describe the most remarkable curves ever conceived by a city engineer. However, these sudden turns are constantly revealing some new and unexpected feature, and one easily forgives the eccentric genius who planed this flowery maze when wandering through its mysterious depths.

Regent street is an exception to the rule, being straight for a half mile or so, and it would be hard to imagine a prettier picture than that presented, looking down this avenue, bordered by waving palms, its white balconied houses half hidden by vines and flowering shrubs, ending at last in a fine grove of mahogany trees, in the midst of which stands the mansion of the govenor.

There are no sidewalks, every one taking the middle of the street, dodging hither and thither to avoid the donkey carts, cabs and horsemen. However, accidents seldom occur, and as there is no mud, and the "Brown Brigade" carefully takes up all dust and papers every morning we need not complain.

Looking in almost any direction we have a background of blue sea with its white caps and hundreds of strange craft, known as dories, but which are peculiar to this locality, being constructed by hollowing out a log, and rigging sloop fashion. These are invaribly manned by caribs who come hundreds of miles to buy and sell in the markets of Belize.

Owing to the prevalence of the trade winds which sweep over

the gulf from the east almost every week during the year, the climate is delightful at all seasons, the summers average about 85 degrees and the winters about 10 degrees lower.

One evening the chief of the fire department called to inquire if I would like to witness his company go through their fortnightly exercises, I told him confidentially that it was for that very purpose that I had left home and kindred and became a wanderer in a strange land. He was much affected, but restrained his feelings remarkably well, though there was a perceptible tremor in his voice as he grasped my hand and said: "It is well' the desire of thy soul shall be granted."

In less than fifteen minutes after it had been announced that the visitor wished to see the "nigger's whoop 'er up" every man was in his place, each arrayed in a flaming red shirt and shining tin helmet.

"Lively now boys," shouted the captain, and the way the old pump rattled down the street was frightful to contemplate. The stentorian tones of the leader were drowned in the chorus of wild yells that rose from the heroic band, as they charged madly along the principal thoroughfare, the rickety old engine lunging from side to side, threatening every moment to start on a deadly excursion through the crowd that lined the way, lending their voices to swell the unearthly din. The machine soon reached the river without accident, other than turning over a fruit stand on top of its terrified owner whose frantics struggles to extricate herself added greatly to the general joy.

A half hour was now spent adjusting the suction house, during which each member acted as leader por tem., giving orders to every one, that no one obeyed; however, all was ready at last. The captain shouted, "Give it to 'er! make 'er howl: shake 'er up lively; let 'er have it!" Thus encouraged each man put his soul in his work and bent to the task as if the salvation of the town depended on his single arm. Shortly the water reached the nozzle, spurting forth fitfully, but gradually increased in force and volume until a distance of thirty-five yard was recorded, which was considered remarkable. I thanked the captain and begged him to dismiss the perspiring crew, who were nearly dead from such unusual exertion.

The town of Belize has been twice destroyed by fire, which

accounts for this department, which is the only one in Central America. The danger is now much less than formerly, owing to the passing of an ordinance prohibiting any but metal or tile roofs.

The town has many pretty churches and a number of large stores, where you can find everything under the sun except the one article you happen to need. Its public buildings are solid, if not elegant, and the market house would do credit to a city of much greater pretensions.

The Belize river divides the town about equally, and is spanned by a bridge over which a motley crowd sweeps from early morning till late at night.

Two weeklies, the Colonial Guardian and Belize Advertiser, supply the news a week after the rest of the world has forgotten it; but the merchants are liberal advertisers, and both publications seem fairly prosperous, and each editor assures me that his paper has a larger circulation than all others combined, which proves that the printers instinct, is much the same the world over.

Belize is a delightful place to spend a few weeks or months during the winter season, the climate during December, January, Februruary and March is simply delightful, while the days are warm the nights are cool enough to make a blanket desirable. Hardly a cloud will be seen during these months, the air is laden with the perfume of flowering plants, pineapples and mangoes abound attaining their greatest perfection, oranges glisten amid the dark green foliage like the fabled apples of gold, and may be had for the picking, providing the owner's away. The private residences of the merchants are furnished with a degree of luxury that astonishes the visitor who has become possessed with the idea that life in the tropics mean simply straw huts and bananas.

The markets furnish almost everything the appetite could wish except fresh butter and milk. These articles are imported in cans, mostly from France or England and answer the purpose very well. Numerous boarding houses and two first class hotels furnish ample accommodation for tourists. The Union Hotel is probably the best known. It was established in 1871 and is pleasantly located on North Front street, surrounded by ample grounds where one may sit in the shade and study the "Tariff" which is printed in English and Spanish as follows:

Precios.		Charge.	
Por Dia	6s	Board and Lodging	6s
Almuerzo O Comida	2s	Breakfast or Dinner	2s
Cafe	1s	Coffee	1s
Posada Solamente	3s	Lodging only	3s
Se Hacen Arreglos Especialls por Messes O Semanas previo Aviso		Arrangements for the month or week to be previously agreed upon.	
I Lainfiesta		Proprietor.	

This information is here inserted free of charge. Mr. Lainfiesta deserves it for maintaining such a comfortable resort at such ridiculously low figures, only 6s Por Dia and then his Almuerzo O Comido is most excellent and very reasonable at 2s. I have personally examined his Posada Solamente and find it perfect in quality and entirely satisfactory as to quantity, in fact no one could expect so large an amount for the trifling sum of 3s.

Within easy reach of Belize are a number of resorts where one may spend a day or two very pleasantly, and a sail over the sparkling waters of the harbor, in the early morning or under the soft light of the moon, is a delightful experience which can be enjoyed at a trifling expense, as the supply of boats and sailors is always equal to the demand. The towns of Livingston and Puerto Cortez are within easy reach by steamer and well repay a visit. The former is the principal port of entree to Guatemala on the Atlantic side and is inhabited for the most part by the Carib Indians, whose strange houses and habits will prove an interesting study. The latter is the principal Atlantic port of Honduras and is connected with San Pedro by the only railroad in the republic. This bit of road is thirty-six miles long, and tourists who wish a novel experience should ride over it. It cost little less than a million dollars a mile and is not paid for. There may be worse roads in the world but they have not been advertised.

There are two great days in Belize. Monday when the mail arrives and Friday when it goes out. As the custom of the country is "never to do anything to-day that can be put off till to-morrow," the consequence is that Friday finds every one answering letters that ought to have been answered on Tuesday, Wednesday or Thursday. Don't speak to anyone now, if you value your life. Wander away to some secluded dell, anywhere to escape the scribbling pen. ·The mail closes at 10 A. M. as the hour approaches the fury increases, to get their letters posted before the fatal stroke of the bell, now becomes the soul ambition of the Belizian, but there is one last hope—a kind, indulgent government, holds the steamer one hour longer during which letters may be taken aboard by paying a double rate. From the income of this last hour, I was told, public buildings were erected, official salaries paid, hospitals and asylums maintained, but I am inclined to think my informant was not strictly reliable, at least not as reliable as I would wish if compiling an Encyclopedia of general information.

BRIDGE AND MARKET HOUSE.

The stranger is struck by the peculiar appearance of the houses and it is sometimes quite a while before he discovers the reason, for as a rule, they are very similar to the buildings at home but after little he looks for the chimneys and finds none. Kitchens are always built separately and at a safe distance from the dwelling. Here the cook reigns, and she is a despot of the most pronounced type. She does not stay at the house but comes at irregular intervals and prepares the meals and departs with the fragments with which she supports her own family and all her near and distant relatives. Servants seldom reside on the premises but come at stated times, each doing the particular work assigned and no more.

As soon as their task is performed they disappear. Every house keeper must have a cook, a table girl, a laundress and one for general house work. Of course, if she lives in any sort of style she will also require a housekeeper: a ladies maid, a butler, coachman, a boy to carry her money and parcels when she goes shopping. These various functionaries appear at certain hours, performing their offices with the slightest possible outlay of energy. Their duties ended they vanish. That's the very word, no other term will describe the suddenness with which they fade away, however, they return next day with less speed and more ceremony, sometimes requiring a full half hour to traverse the space between the gate to the door, but they file up promptly Saturday and take their wages with just as much satisfaction as though they had earned it. The servant does all the marketing and thereby increases her salary perceptably—for instance you tell cook to get "fip-pence worth o' plantains," she will return with a pennyworth and explain the small measure by a long story about low market. "Plantain mighty scase Missus. Most all gone fur true. Bockra man just get all," and so with everything else, Bockra is the Carib word for white. From time immemorial the native cook has prepared the meals on a primitive range made by placing a couple of stones on the floor then laying another across for a top, and when some of the more enterprising merchants sought to introduce modern stoves there was a regular "howl." However, they were gradually adopted. A friend of ours had just put one in and had, as she supposed, explained its workings so that the cook would have no trouble. You can imagine her astonishment when, after waiting an hour and a half for dinner, she ventured to investigate the cause of delay to find the demon of the kitchen standing over the stove fairly boiling with rage, and pouring forth a perfect torrent of Creole English mixed with a large proportion Carib Spanish, the only language in which she could express the heavy weight "swear words" with which she was freighted; instead of starting the fire in the stove she had kindled a huge conflagration under it, then placed the victuals on top, in the oven, in the fire place, on the hearth and "there she stood yelling like a wounded tiger" said my friend, and "when she saw me laughing, turned with a bread knife in such fury that I was glad to escape to the house." After a few weeks the poor creature became reconciled but insists to this day that the old style is much the best and to prove her wisdom makes a practice of burning up a dinner about once a week.

I have spoken of the stores where are kept "everything except the article you want." Perhaps I ought to modify that remark, for on several occasions I found exactly what I was looking for and was surprised to note the great amount and variety of goods handled by these merchants, whose trade extends hundreds of miles along the coast and far back into the interior towns of Guatemala and Honduras. Among the establishments as vast and varied as a museum, I might mention Beattie & Co., of the "Colosseum," James Brodie & Co., A. E. Morlan, the largest dealer in jewelry, musical instruments and merchandise in Central America. Here you will find all the latest novelties imported direct from the manufacturers in England and Europe as well as the United States. The owner of this establishment is also United States Consul* for this port which, of course, makes his store the center of attraction to tourists from the states, who are speedily attracted to the spot by the stars and stipes which floats above the office. Among other representatives houses might be mentioned B. Cramer & Co., Krug & Oswald, Gray & Co.

The stranger will find a mine of amusement in the market, which he may work at intervals to good advantage. Here he will meet a busy throng, noisy but good-natured, every one trying to get the best of every one else in the way of trade. Caribs from the adjacent coast with their little stores of fruit, Casava Bread, yams, plantains, etc., Coolies from India squatting on the ground with their stock in trade arranged on mats before them. These people have a peculiar, far away, melancholy expression that is touching to note, but I'm told they are about the shrewdest traders in the market. Indians, half-breeds, Chinese and Mexicans mingle in this strange crowds and urge their wares with such vehemence of gesture and wealth of language that it takes a man of strong mental qualities to be able to run this gauntlet of attractions without carrying away some memento of the place.

---

*Since the above was written, Mr. Morlan's establishment has changed hands, Mr. N. J. Keating succeeding to the business. However, the office of the U. S. Consulate will be found in its old quarters immediately East of the store.

The inhabitants depend altogether on rain water for all domestic purposes, each house being provided with a huge tank for preserving the same and on a public square near the center of the city a collection of huge wooden reservoirs will be seen. These huge barrells, 20 or 25 feet high, 50 or 60 feet in circumference, always attract the attention of the visitor. They are the property of the colony and are used as a reserve supply on which the citizens may draw in times of drought. Naturally this water is very warm but is rendered cool by a simple process. Each family is provided with a large stone jar of porous texture with a slim neck, locally known as a "water monkey." These are filled and placed where a current of air will strike them and it is remarkable how soon the contents become cool and palatable.

BARRACKS.

One of the pleasant features of Belize is "The Colonial Club," which was established in 1880. This association includes in its membership all the literary and artistic talent of the place, and to its influence, direct and otherwise, we may trace much of the improvement that has marked the past ten years of the cities history. The Club took possession of its handsome and pleasant quarters on Regent street, January 15, 1886, and is open every day, Sundays excepted. The Reading Rooms, Library and Billiard Parlors are on the third floor over looking the bay, from whence comes a delightful breeze. Strangers are welcome, and they will find here all the leading publications of the United States and England, besides a library that will surprise you by the large number and excellent character of books contained, which includes many of the standard historical and scientific works, as well as late editions of the encyclopedias, dictionaries, etc. To these are added a respectable collection of the lighter literature of the day, largely English, of course, but containing a fair sprinkling of American authors.

On the second floor is a large hall where the literary branch of the association hold their meetings and at times indulge in amatuer theatricals. These performances are sure to attract a large audience, which, if it is disappointed by the exibition, never acknowledge it, because its "quite English you know."

Mention has already been made of the healthfulness of this port; there are other than natural advantages that account for the immunity from fevers enjoyed by the residents of Belize, these are found in the strict sanitary regulations enforced by the officers entrusted with that most responsible department of the colonial government.

Through the efforts of this body almost perfect drainage has been attained by a system of canals, that carry off all surface water, and which, aside from their value in a sanitary point of view, are made an ornament to the city, the sides and bottom being smoothly cemented, and handsomely curbed throughout their length with the same indestructible material; they are lined with flowering shrubs, and over hung by masses of foilage, all being reflected in the glassy surface with the accuracy of a mirror and the streets are carried over by numerous bridges producing an affect that is charming as well as novel.

It is gratifying to know that the death rate has been greatly lowered by these precautions, since the completion of this work, yellow fever has almost dissapeared while ague and malarial complaints have been reduced to the minimum, in fact Belize, at the present time will compare favorably in the matter of health statistics, with towns of similar size in the States, which enjoy very much greater climatic advantages.

Like all towns, Belize has its children of genius, "natural born" poets, painters, inventors, mind readers, etc., etc., these local celebrities are pointed out to the visitor and their various accomplishments, paraded with a degree of pride that is comendable. While loafing around one of the newspaper offices one day the editor placed a bundle of papers in my hands labeled "offerings of the

Poets." It had been accumulating for months, they did not strike him as being quite the thing for a newspaper, but he has pacified the writers by promising to publish the collection in a neat volume, under the title of "colonial songs, by colonial songsters," as soon as time will permit. As he hopes to be busy for several years to come he kindly allowed me to copy a few of the most touching, which are here given. Not, however, as a fair example of Belizian literature, but rather as a tropical curiosity.

ODE TO SIR JOHN CROW.

Sir John Crow sat on a potato tree
Picking his teeth so silently, silently,
His good wife sat right by his side
Gazing o'er the sea so wild and wide.
Said he to she, "what d'ye think,"
Said she to he, "let's take a drink."
Then Sir John flapped his sable wing,
"You bet, that's just the proper thing."

G. G. S———n.

TO LUCINDA JANE.

O beautiful girl, with the dark black curl
I'm waiting for thee by the deep, damp sea,
Waiting for thee, waiting for thee,
All alone by the moist wet sea.

Then quickly come, and bring your gum
And we will chin, while the minutes spin.
For my arm is long and my heart is strong,
Then hurry along, love, hurry along.

J. D. L———d.

(*Last and best.*)

EVENING IN BELIZE.

"The sand fly floats in the evening air,
The mosquito, too, is everywhere,
Other bugs and things that sting
Are crawling over everything,
    Everything—Everything.
Soap and candles
Sugar and snuff,
Land of lizards and plumduff."

F. C. Mc———l.

CHAPTER II.

AT THE AMERICAN HOTEL—A CARIB VILLAGE—HISTORICAL SKETCH OF THE STRANGE PEOPLE—A FUNERAL—SAIL ON THE RIO DULCE—ARRIVE AT SANTA THOMAS.

Having concluded our work in Belize, we took our departure for the South on the evening of May 4. On the morning of the fifth we found ourselves in the Harbor of Puerto Cortez, with the lofty mountain of Omoa on our right and the village on the left, which looked very pretty from a distance, half hidden among the shadows of the tall trees. But a closer view revealed but few passably decent houses with a large number of old frames, that were all but ready to fall, a few thatched huts, a sandy waste called a street, through which the celebrated railroad is built, a custom house which I hope has fallen down or been blown away or otherwise destroyed, but no doubt it is tottering in its old track to this day—changes rarely occur in this country, only one or two have been noted since its discovery in 1502.

Our vessel lay here several hours taking on bananas, five thousand bunches were received, about one-fourth that number were rejected and cast into the sea, much to the disgust of the producers. Next morning found us at Livingston, which, as has already been stated is Guatemala's chief port of entry on the Atlantic coast. Here we found accommodation at the "American Hotel" kept by Mr. J. C. Norrich. The "American" is not as large as the Astor House, but it is more expensive in proportion to its size, "Tariff" $2.00 per diem. If the Astor House should take the American as a standard and charge in the same ratio for service rendered, I judge its rates would be about $60,000 a week, however, the American furnishes many things that would be a novelty at the Astor. The frijoles are just as good as anybody's and weigh just as much to the pound. Here we first met the tortillas with which we afterward became so familiar. Now we might have lived at the Astor for years and never made the acquaintance of either of these nutritious dishes. The "American" has fewer rooms than the Astor but accommodates more guests. These guests do not all leave their autographs in the register. In order to have more space for our work we hired a house across the street, where we established our headquarters from whence the writer made daily excursion into the surrounding forrests, while his more methodical and business-like companion arranged a glittering exhibition that attracted crowds of natives from all the country round.

Livingston contains a large Carib population which proved an interesting study. In the following paper, which was originally published in the Indianapolis Journal, the writer endeavored to give a brief outline of their history as told by "Jim" with some observation on their present habits and condition.

"During my recent visit to Guatemala I became greatly interested in that strange race, now nearly extinct, known as the Carib Indians. The village of Livingston, situated at the entrance of the Gulf Dulce, is one of the largest settlements of these people, containing, as near as I could learn, about two thousand Caribs,

AMERICAN HOTEL, LIVINGSTON.

with a few whites and a handful of soldiers, ragged, barefooted and totally undisciplined, but whose presence is deemed necessary to maintain the dignity of the little republic and properly impress the stranger with the military resources of the country. Being delayed some time at this place, the writer devoted his leisure hours to the study of Carib history from their own standpoint, but, must I admit it, with small success, for, garrulous as they are on almost any other subject, they could hardly be induced to speak of themselves: however, by putting together the fragments gleaned from different sources, I think the reader may get a very fair idea of the present condition of this remnant of a once powerful race, with a glimpse of its past record that may prove interesting to those whose tastes lead them in the direction of historical research or the more delightful study of folk lore. This singular reticence in regard to their customs and beliefs may be accounted for, in part, from the dread they have of being interfered with by the government, whose representatives regard with suspicion the performance of certain rights and ceremonies held sacred by the successors of the fiery Caonabo, who reigned in the southern archipelago at the time of its discovery by Columbus.

In the writer's opinion, these periodical complaints are simply the result of jealousy on the part of the petty officials, whose envy is aroused by the superior thrift of the Caribs, whose industrious and economical habits contrast sharply with the lazy, shiftless lives of the half-breeds, who are in many instances appointed to administer the law in these remote corners of the state, and whose fitness for the position is never questioned, providing their political creed is found favorable to the party in power. It is a matter of astonishment that a people of such primitive habits should have survived the terrible persecution of the Spaniards, whose heartless cruelty seemed satisfied with nothing short of the total extinction of every national trait, as witness the Aztecs of Mexico, and the still more highly cultured "Children of the Sun," who had converted the desert wastes of Peru into blooming gardens, and whose knowledge of agriculture and mechanics should have been preserved at all hazards, as an acquisition of far greater importance, than all the mineral wealth of the mountains. Had thirst for knowledge equaled her love of gold, Spain might to-day have held the first place among the nations of the earth, but, like all nations or individuals whose highest aim is the accumulation of wealth for purely selfish ends, the successors of Ferdinand and Isabella sank steadily, until, at the present time, they occupy the lowest position among the powers laying claim to any degree of civilization.

But my present purpose is not to discuss questions or morality or philosophy, but rather to sketch hastily some of the characteristics of this interesting tribe, whose ancestors ruled the Western sea, and whose huge, painted dories appearing on the horizon filled the inhabitants of the neighboring islands with consternation. The Caribs of to-day are confined to a few small settlements along the coast of Honduras, and at this one point in Guatemala, they have not only retained their native tongue, but many of their ancient customs, and continue to be the best sailors on the coast. They were first met with by Columbus on his second voyage, and formed a striking contrast to the friendly, easy-going savages with whom he became familiar during his first visit. Among all the daring enterprises undertaken by the Admiral, or those under his command, the ones directed against these ferocious chiefs were attended with the most danger, and the story of the wild adventures of the valiant Ojeda reads more like Grecian fable than actual historical facts. However, their desperate courage, coupled with a knowledge of war far superior to that of the tribes around them, was no match for their civilized assailants, and their story from that time is one of gradual decay. Driven from point to point by an ever advancing foe, the territory of the Carib Chiefs rapidly dwindled away until their identity as a nation was lost; in 1796 the English government transported the entire Carib population from Dominica and St. Vincent to Ruatan, a small but fertile island near the coast of Honduras, whither most of them have since emigrated, owing to the constant encroachment of English settlers.

MANGROVE TREE.

These people have a legend, somewhat shady, but pretty withal, which I drew from an old Carib sailor locally known as

"Jim," in whose dory I spent many pleasant hours, skirting the palm-fringed shores of the Rio Dulce, as the natives persist in calling the narrow entrance to Lake Golfete. This story necessarily abridged for present purposes, traces their history back through centuries of time to the cradle of the nation in a beautiful valley in the midst of the Blue mountains of North America, and corresponding with the territory now known as Virginia or North Carolina. In this happy vale, surrounded by every luxury an Indian could desire, they lived and loved, fought and died, and were buried or burned, as the case might be; the rich bottom lands furnished corn in abundance, almost without effort, the mountains were alive with game, the rivers swarmed with fish, the men were brave, the women beautiful, and there they might have been living in peace and happiness to this day, possibly, had not a most unfortunate vision come to their chief, Un-gow-a, in which a lovely female formed the central feature, as is frequently the case in visions of to-day among men much further advanced socially and politically.

This figure, as described by the infatuated Un-gow-a, posssessed a fair skin, a face radiant with light, while her long golden tresses floated about her shapely shoulders like a cloud. She appeared every evening in the southern sky, smiling and beckoning to our unhappy chief. True, others saw nothing but a bright star, with a long trail of light streaming after it, but no Carib ever questioned a chief, especially on matters connected with visions in which handsome women appeared. It wasn't considered safe. So the lovely phantom appearing every evening, continued to smile and beckon, until Un-gow-a quite lost his head, if not his heart, and, like men of a much later period, soon found a hundred or more good and sufficient reasons for doing the thing he most of all desired to do. He, therefore, assembled the wise men in common council, during which he delivered an address of such persuasive eloquence and convincing power that each member of that conservative body expressed himself more than satisfied with the plan suggested, which was nothing less than the abandoning of their mountain home to follow the bright star of the southern sky, for it was as such that the beautiful creature appeared to ordinary eyes. Un-gow-a told them by so doing they would be led to a land of flowers, where snow would never be seen, where would be found fruits of every kind flourishing throughout the year, where cold and hunger, work and worry would be forgotten, in fact he drew a picture so fascinating in detail, so rich in coloring and poetic in sentiment that the whole tribe was wild with delight, with the exception of two old sceptics, who were promptly burned. This pleasant duty ended, the nation demanded to be led forthwith to the land of rest and ready-made hominy.

Thus began the long series of moves to the southward, lured on from year to year by the bright vision that still smiled encouragingly, shaking her shining tresses over the soft summer sky at that witching hour, between daylight and dark, when even ordinary objects are invested with a strange charm. On they went, fighting

OLDEST CHURCH IN AMERICA, ISLAND OF COZUMEL.

their way through hostile territories, climbing mountains, fording rivers, cutting paths through matted jungles, conquering all foes, overcoming all obstacles, until at last they found themselves confronted by a wild waste of water. Great minds are only stimulated by opposition. These doughty warriors gazed awhile on the heaving deep and decided to cross it, and to that end began at once the construction of a boat suitable for the purpose. This was the first of the famous dories which have excited the admiration of all sailors down to the present day. With their usual good fortune they passed safely to the nearest island of that long chain now known as the Bahamas. Thereafter their progress was an uninterrupted series of conquests, passing from one verdant isle to another until they reached the great archipelago of the southern Antilles, where every promise of the beautiful guide seemed fulfilled and the vision faded from the sky, not, however, until she had made an earthward swoop, carrying off the faithful Un-gow-a to shine with her forever in some remote heaven for beyond the ken of mortals. Here in these lovely islands, shaded by stately groves, watered by crystal springs, the weary warriors built their villages. Surely this was the Indian paradise, the veritable "happy hunting ground." Fruits to every taste, flowers of every hue, serene skies, sunny seas, misty mountains, limpid streams, vast forests, where bright-winged birds flashed from tree, or poised on the perfumed air, their trembling wings sparkling like gems in the sunlight. Such, in short, is the story of the Caribs, as told by "Jim," which, no doubt, is quite as false and not more foolish than the fables of the Norsemen, which have fed the insatiable appetites of a dozen generations of poets, without affecting these inexhaustable minds of fiction.

Improbable as this story of Carib migration may seem, it has engaged the serious attention of a number of learned writers, among whom might be mentioned the name of our own Irving, who, referring to some similar fable says: "To trace the footsteps of this roving tribe throughout its wide migrations from the Appalachian Mountains along the clusters of islands which stud the Gulf of Mexico and Carribean Sea, to the shores of Paria and so across the vast regions of Guayana and Amazonia to the remote coast of Brazil, would be one of the most curious researches in aboriginal history and throw much light on the mysterious question of the population of the New World;" and it must remain a matter of regret that this most delightful of American historical writers was never moved to undertake the work.

While the Caribs of to-day are regarded with suspicion by a certain class of people, those who know them best will tell you that they are not only industrious, but in most cases honest and trustworthy; that some of the men have a weakness for rum cannot be denied, but in a country where this beverage forms a part, and often the principal part of every merchant's stock, it is not a matter of surprise that some have followed the example of their white neighbors. The women are hard workers, earning good wages on the sugar and banana plantations, where their services are always in demand, while many who reside in the villages engage in the laundry business; one of the sights of Livingston is this department of Carib enterprise. Near the landing, where a strong spring furnishes an abundant supply of clear, soft water, you can see almost any day a half dozen or more women bending over little wooden troughs made by splitting a small tree in halves and hewing out the insides, just as the northern farmers do when short of "sap" buckets during maple sugar season. They use no "washboards," but saturate the clothes with soap and water, after which they beat them over large, smooth stones, with disastrious results sometimes. They present a highly picturesque appearance with their single sleeveless garment, which is cut very low in the neck, and greatly abridged in length, and is held in place by shoulder straps. This feminine invention, which cannot be properly described as a "dress" or a "skirt," or even as a "waist," forms their sole protec-

BELIZE, FROM THE BAY.

tection from the burning rays of the tropical sun, excepting the red or yellow turbans worn more as an ornament than from any necessity.

The men are nearly all sailors, and are either employed on the coasting vessels or as lightermen, or as is frequently the case, engaged in the carrying trade independently, many of them owning dories of several tons burden, which they manage with remarkable skill. These boats are models of their kind. They are constructed of a solid piece of wood, hollowed and shaped with the greatest care. They are all sizes, from the tiniest craft capable of carrying only one or two persons, up to thirty or forty feet in length, with a carrying capacity of twelve to fifteen tons. We frequently met these little shells several miles from shore with a single occupant standing up and steering his course with the utmost ease. Sometimes when the sea was rough both man and boat would disappear behind a huge roller, always, however, rising on the next wave, where it would hang an instant on the crest, then down like an arrow into the watery valley. To us it seemed quite impossible for such frail specks to survive in the wild tumult of wind and waves, but these intrepid sailors showed no concern whatever, but hailed us cheerily as they passed and were soon lost in the distance. Often in the dusk of evening these strange rovers of the deep would appear suddenly, like restless spirits wandering abroad over the dark waters, their swarthy features illumined an instant by the rudy glow of the ship's lantern, and then swallowed up in the gloom.

As already stated these boats are constructed of one solid piece of wood and the building of one of the larger sizes is an undertaking of great importance, the first step, of course, is the selection of a suitable tree. This frequently involves a search through miles of forest and occupies weeks of time. The largest vessel of this class, that came under my notice, and which I carefully measured, proved to be a little over eight feet across the beam and sixty feet in length. The reader can imagine the size of the tree from which this huge dory was cut. However, it was not considered a good model, being twelve or fourteen feet too short to meet the nice requirements of the native draughtsman. The dwellings of the Caribs also attract attention by their peculiar construction, being almost identical with those found on the islands at the time of their discovery. No nails are used, the frame being secured by lashings of the rope like vines with which the forests abound. In this way each plate and rafter is fastened. Then comes the roof. This is made of the huge fronds of the Cahune palms, ingeniously woven together, and when completed will effectually turn the heavy rains that fall daily during the wet season. The walls of these unique houses are made by weaving together a kind of wild cane, like rude basket work. In some cases these are plastered over with mud, but oftener left open, and lively scenes are sometimes witnessed during the evening hours when the interior is illuminated by the pine torches or the fire on the floor over which the good wife prepares the evening meal which she and her lord will enjoy separately, as the wife never presumes to eat at the same table with her husband. They have a fable which pretends to account for this unsocial custom by stating that at a remote period the Caribs captured their women from a neighboring tribe and made them their wives without the usual formality, which so enraged the sensitive creatures that they vowed never to associate with their captors as companions, though compelled to follow them as servants.

THE LAUNDRY.

These dwellings, viewed from a distance, so exactly resemble huge stacks of hay that the writer had often been deceived by the appearance, and even after a long residence in the country, would still find himself surprised to see a thin blue column of smoke slowly rising from their crests, betraying the secret of the interior. These abodes are built so closely together in villages that frequently the low projecting eaves actually touch, leaving only two or three feet between walls. They are placed at all angles without the least regard for the cardinal points. While the walls are only six or seven feet high at the sides, the roof towers up twenty-five or thirty feet. Usually they have but two openings, one at the front, the other at the rear end. These are sometimes closed by a wicket gate, but oftener are left open day and night. As might be expected where such inflamable structures are built so closely, fires sometimes occur, but as a rule one or two houses only are destroyed, for contrary to appearance, these thatched roofs burn very slowly and are easily extinguished. This is owing to the fact that they are very compactly woven, to a thickness of 12 to 16 inches, and during the wet season become so saturated with water that they hardly get dry before the recurrance of the rainy months. In case of such disaster, the inhabitants turn out enmasse, and rebuild the destroyed house, without any thought of recompense, so that aside from the temporary inconvenience, the loss is not felt.

The Carib housewife is easily satisfied so far as house furnishings are concerned. A small table, two or three stools from the native workshop, usually complete her outfit. The stove consists of a couple of stones, over which a third of flat shape is laid. Under this the fire is built on the earthen floor. The smoke finds its way out through crevices in roof and wall. Bedsteads are unknown, the hammock forming their only couch. But if the Carib wife or daughter care little for carpets, chairs, or dresses, they make up this deficiency in the feminine character, by their inordinate craving for jewelry, no woman considering herself fully dressed without at least a necklace of gold or silver, while if her means will allow she will fairly weigh herself down with earrings, bracelets, and strings of beads, to say nothing of finger rings, lockets, chains and charms. Enterprising traders knowing their weakness in this direction, visit their villages from time to time and are always sure of a good trade, at least as long as their money holds out. At the time of my visit one of these Nomadic dealers appeared and opened a store in a deserted house and I spent some time watching them trade, often admiring the tact displayed, in order to secure the coveted article at a price which they considered a bargain. They imagine they can detect an alloy in metals by the sense of smell and we were often amused to see both men and women subjecting the different articles in the case to this curious test. We were also surprised with what accuracy they were able to judge of the merits of pieces that appeared exactly alike to the eye. Several times the jeweler tested this faculty by taking two rings, one solid, the other plated, and between which we could see no difference. These he wrapped in tissue paper, leaving only a small surface of the metal visible, then holding them in his own hand, submit them for inspection, asking "which good?" The answer usually came promptly and was nearly always correct.

The wearing apparel of the men rivals that of the women in simplicity, consisting of a pair of pants made of cotton drill, to which on state occasions may be added a shirt of the same material. The pants are held in place by a leathern belt with a holder for the inseparable "Machete," a long, heavy knife which is used for every conceivable purpose. In the cultivation of their crops, this universal tool takes the place of plow, harrow, hoe and rake, while in the household it represents the can opener, butcher knife,

THE DOCTOR DISCHARGED.

hatchet, hammer, ax, saw or plane. I doubt if any other people can turn one tool to as many uses and do it as gracefully. Carib language is a terror to strangers to whom it seems the wildest gibberish, though we were told that it has been reduced to a system, provided with a well defined grammar, and that some pious priests once published a prayer book in the native tongue, though we failed to discover a copy.

To the traveler who hears it for the first time it is simply an unintelligible jumble, and seems to be complete in less than a dozen words, or rather sounds, which are continually repeated with fiery vehemence. In this connection I may be excused for quoting this passage from a recently published letter, "Their language is as peculiar as their dress and manners, and is exceedingly hard to master. The laundress has just called and rendered her bill orally in the following flowery strain:

"Iugowalibouswabt uzomel Erugubas evtre yeloken of spachedruz! Is it any wonder we look forward to every funeral with a sort of wild exultation?

An amusing incident occured during our stay at Livingston, which proved very disagreeable to one of the parties concerned. A young German but recently arrived and quite ignorant of Carib customs secured passage in one of their boats bound for Belize. Everything went well until evening, when the captain made for a lonely headland, covered with a dense forest of palms. Here they made a landing and soon had a good fire with a large kettle swinging over it. At times they indulged in a strange dance around the fire accompanied by the wildest gestures and most doleful chant. Our German friend watched their performance from his place in the boat with ever-increasing apprehension, but when the crew returned presently and invited him to join them on shore he became thoroughly scared. In their ignorance of his language they tried to make him understand by signs that supper was ready. They would point to their mouths, all the while working their jaws rapidly, then shut their eyes, which meant simply, that after eating they would sleep and continue the journey in the morning, but their passenger, whose mind was filled with wild fancies, interpreted their friendly overtures quite differently. He imagined he was to be killed and cooked; and not being in sympathy with the plan, finally covered the leader with his revolver, it was the Caribs turn to be frightened now, and with one accord they disappeared under the water, for they swim like porpoises, some coming up at the bow served to attract his attention by pretending to climb up by the cable, while two others silently slipped over the stern and quickly disarmed the trembling Dutchman, following this act by tying him securely and in this condition he was delivered next day, half starved, to the authorities at Belize. Interpreters were called and the story soon unraveled; from the remarkable actions of the German, the natives supposed him to be a lunatic, and so did the very best thing under the circumstances. Mutual explanations, followed by a square meal and a case of rum for the wearied crew, made everything alright and diplomatic relations between two great powers remained undisturbed.

I cannot bring this article to a close without recording a most emphatic denial of the charge of Cannibalism, which has sometimes been preferred against the Caribs, by persons entirely ignorant of their habits and history. The fact is, the Carib population of Honduras, is far the most desirable of all the different tribes represented in the colony. As a rule, they are harmless, good natured, industrious and remarkable cleanly, a virtue, by the way, almost unknown among the Indians and half-breeds of the interior. The writer will always remember his visit among these dusky descendants of the wild sea rovers, with pleasure. The name recalls many a dash among the roaring breakers, many a campfire on the lonely shore, followed by a substantial lunch with its dessert of juicy pineapples or still more delicious mangoes, then to our hammocks to smoke and gossip and watch the stars or listen to the waves, until one by one the pipes went out, and we slept as only tired travelers could."

One warm afternoon we were aroused from our siesta by a discordant jingling of bells and supposing a fire had broken out we made a rush for the street, when the landlady informed us that it was only a funeral, and said it would pass the house. A few minutes later, hearing a sort of wild music mingled with shouts and laughter, we hurried to the balcony where we arrived just in time to see four half drunk men, shoeless and hatless, coming along at a brisk pace bearing a coffin on their shoulders. It was simply a rough box wrapped in a piece of stripped calico and swayed from side to side as the bearers reeled along. Following was a woman, the widow I was told, carrying a rude cross covered with flowers. She seemed in excellent spirits and was laughing immoderately. Next to the hilarious chief mourner came the band, consisting of one accordian, two fiddles, a tin horn and a drum. All were running to their full capacity, following the band came a mixed crowd of men, women and children. The men were attired in their usual costume, a pair of cotton drawers, and shirt worn outside. The women were simply dressed, with the regulation sleeveless garment, that shows their dusky charms to such good advantage. The children were arrayed in their innocence only. All, from the least to the greatest were smoking and all laughed and danced by turns. It was by all odds the most cheerful and inspiring funeral we had ever witnessed. I had just returned to my desk when my attention was once more called to the street by a chorus of yells and uproarious merriment. Stepping out, the cause was apparent. One of the bearers had stumbled and fallen, throwing the coffin to the ground, one side of the frail box was broken out, exposing an arm and a ghastly hand half closed; but it was a well behaved corpse, and instead of getting out and thrashing the awkard bearers, as it should have done, it simply lay quiet taking the whole thing as a joke. Presently the fallen man struggled to his feet. The coffin was again taken up and the procession moved merrily on. The landlord declared that this was a very tame affair and assured us that the burial services of the rich are very much livlier and more imposing—in such cases the "body" is dressed up in the best shirt his estate affords. It is then carefully tied in a chair in an upright position and thus carried to the grave

BARRACKS LIVINGSTON.

yard while the whole town turns out to do him honor by the discharge of crackers, rockets and a variety of native fire works, while the drinking is general and the joy unbounded.

We hoped to witness a first-class affair, but were dissapointed by the unreasonable stubborness of the principle, he was the owner of three huts and a pair of mules, a regular Jay Gould, and he was sick enough to die—everybody said so—and everybody was looking forward to a grand time, yet this hard hearted unsympathizing creature refused to abandon his real estate and live stock, and even had the audacity to discharge his doctor, after which he rapidly recovered. It was several days, however, before he took this bold step and it was during this time that his friends exhibited so much anxiety. They would steal up to the door to note progress and report to the eager crowd. The interest was intense. As usual in times of great excitement, the news was very conflicting; one bulletin was to the effect that he was almost gone; at such times a confused murmur would run through the assembly and an occasional shout would be heard, with here and there a random cracker. Then would come some discouraging news, he was getting better, slowly but steadily growing stronger, and faces bright with happy anticipations became clouded by dissapointment. Finally a committee was appointed to wait upon the sick man. They argued the case long and well but he was obdurate. They had to give up. After while they returned, they came in great haste. The miserable millionaire, with the cold indifference of the class he represents the world over, not only stubbornly refused to give his humble fellow citizens a brief half holiday, but actually drove them off the premises with a club. It was then that he discharged the doctor and all hope was abandoned. The following note on "oysters" is taken from our memorandum book, and recalls an incident of a somewhat novel character.

"We went oyster hunting this morning had fairly good success—James knocked them off the trees, while the rest of us gathered them up—got about two bushels—they were fat and plump—but not large; they roost on trees but not very high—they do not fly.

This was a novel experience—always thought oysters lived in the water—never heard of them being found on trees—learn something every day—this is literally true—the shores are lined with mangrove trees, these trees are very peculiar, they flourish in salt water, they are about equally divided between roots and branches, the former strike out from about 10 or 12 feet above the water reaching down at an angle of 45 degrees, much resembling the skeleton of an umbrella half closed, the branches shoot up in much the same manner, making a 'tree 40 feet high—the oysters attach themselves to these roots when the tide is in, when it ebbs they are left high and dry, and all the hunter has to do is to gather them like any other fruit—at a little distance, a grove of mangroves has the appearance of a forest on stilts, while single trees look like leafy giants wading in the sea."

Messers. Anderson and Owen represent the interests of the United States at this point. Both stand high in commercial circles and are known far and wide. These gentlemen did much to make our stay in Livingston pleasant and profitable. Mr. Anderson was so charmed with the climate that he declared he would never live anywhere else, and as an evidence of his sincerity, he had erected one of the finest private residences on the coast. The situation was certainly delightful, on the crest of a high hill, overlooking the village and bay on the left, on the right the eye wandered over the mountain heights that rose beyond the famed Rio Dulce, a description of which formed the subject of a letter to the "Pittsburg Post" which I take the liberty to borrow.

"I have just returned from a trip up the Rio Dulce, which is claimed by some to be the most beautiful river in the world, (the Rio Dulce, so called, is not a river at all, but a long narrow body of water known as Lake Golfete, which connects the larger lake known as Gulf Dulce, with the Gulf of Honduras, but it is just as pretty as though it was a river and, in fact is usually spoken of as such.) One traveler speaking on the subject, said he had traversed Europe and America in search of the picturesque, visiting almost every place celebrated in song and story on both continents, and his sketch book contained many lovely bits from sunny France, Spain and Italy. He dwelt long in Switzerland and carried thence many beautiful studies, but for restful, dreamy, intoxicating beauty, he acknowledged the Rio Dulce queen of all. It may not be amiss to state that this charming bit of water is situated in the eastern part of Guatemala and forms the boundary line between the departments of Chiquimula and Vera Paz. Its general course is north-east and its outlet the Gulf of Honduras. A small steamer makes weekly trips between Livingston near the mouth, to Isabel a small Spanish settlement near the head of navigation. Having heard so much regarding the scenery along this stream, I determined to view it for myself. I, therefore, consulted a friend and we decided to take the excursion together. We, looked about and found a boat that would answer very well, also a stout Carib to man it. With a well-filled hamper, we stepped on board just as day was breaking. The morning was perfect, and under the influence of a scarcely perceptible breeze we moved slowly up stream, beneath the shadows of the mountains which rise abruptly from the eastern shore, watching the gradual lighting of the opposite range, whose highest points rises far above the clouds and whose misty summits are bathed in the warm sunlight fully an hour before the denser forests at their feet.

Nothing could be more delightful than to float thus idly along, lying at our ease, watching the shifting shadows every moment giving way before the king of day. The water is so clear one could easily imagine the boat suspended in air. At a depth of six fathoms the river's floor was plainly seen, covered with pebbles and bright colored shells. Fish of many varieties were darting from place to place like flashes of light. Others lazily suspended in the crystal depths watched us we imagined, with a degree of curiosity quite equal to our own.

The shore is covered with white sand and pebbles up to the tide limit, where the rich tropical vegetation begins, which for luxuriance and variety is probably unexcelled. Right above the

MODERN RANGE.

white line of the beach we have the pimento, rancoon and cahune palms, massed together with trees of a hundred varieties, the whole over run with a tangled mass of vines and creepers, many of them laden with brilliant flowers, among which we noted the morning glory, the only familiar face among this wild confusion of green and crimson.

At six o'clock our man ran the Dory ashore on a wide stretch of white sand, where a cool spring added its limpid waters to the river. Here he started a fire and proceeded to make a cup of coffee and spread a light lunch. A campfire has a charm all its own, the flickering blaze, the column of blue smoke slowly rising and spreading out among the tops of the trees; the odor of frying ham, the cheerful simmering of the coffee pot are never so enticing as when encountered in the forest, remote from the haunts of men. There was a Sabbath-like stillness, broken only by the song of birds and the gentle purling of the brook as it made its way over the shinning sands. Among the bird voices only one was familiar, that of the morning dove, filling the air with its sweet, but melancholy strain.

Our repast over, we re-enter the boat. The wonderful panorama increases in interest and beauty at every turn. The breeze has freshened and the dory glides swiftly along at the base of the mountains, whose seared summits tower a mile above us, in places presenting almost perpendicular walls a thousand feet high. Over these frowning ramparts nature has thrown a veil of swaying vines and flowering shrubs, whose many colored blossoms relieve the vivid green of the overhanging foliage. We note beds of lillies of several different species, among them one that closely resembles the calla. On the higher slopes are the wild fruit trees, some bursting forth in a gorgeous array of white and pink, others laden with golden clusters ripening in the sun.

Thus we float on in a trance of delight, passing point after point, each new opening revealing some hidden treasure. We take no thought of time or toil, free for the moment, as the birds of the forest whose liquid notes come across the waters faintly, like music in a dream. At times the river widens out to a lake-like proportion. Here and there are little islands so lovely in their solitude that one could almost wish to give up the world with its thousand cankering cares and stop among these enchanted bowers for ever more.

What an existence! To open one's eyes every morning on such a display of color, such effects of light and shade, such vistas framed by jutting headlands that stretch away interminably until the outlines are gradually lost in the violet haze that no painter may attempt or poet describe. Oh, thou disconsolate lover, forego thy piteous sighs! Here is a retreat suited to thy condition. Kind nature will murmur in thy ear sweet sympathy. Every voice of earth and air will minister to thy comfort and fill thy heart with a deep content.

At noon our guide turned the boat into a little bay which proved to be the mouth of a mountain stream that came tumbling over the rocks in noisy glee, sparkling in the sunlight as it danced over the white pebbles of the shore. In this pleasant nook we tarried an hour, sketching and lunching by turns. Near by a pair of pelicans set us a noble example by their unflagging industry. They made their headquarters on a projecting rock, from whence they took excursions up and down or across the river, seldom returning without a fish, which they caught by droping suddenly on the unsuspecting victim.

At one place a boiling spring rises from the bottom of the stream with such force that the surface of the water is raised a couple of feet or more above the general level, and the sound of escaping steam is fearfully suggestive of possible eruption. Large

LIVELY FUNERAL, LIVINGSTON.

fragments of pumice stone abound, showing conclusively that at one time this peaceful region must have echoed to the dreadful sounds of bursting volcanoes and devastating earthquakes.

During the afternoon we returned, very reluctanly and slowly, now on one shore, now across to the other, exploring bays, discoving waterfalls, some of considerable extent, whose merry music runs on through the whole year unchecked by winter's frost or summer's drouth.

About three o'clock we were overtaken by one of those showers that arise so suddenly in this latitude, but our worthy guide was not to be surprised. Warned by signs of which we were quite ignorant, he made for a little cove, sheltered on the windward side by a towering wall of rock, where he dropped anchor, and in less than five minutes stretched a water proof awning that completely protected us from the rain. But it was quickly over, and the sun striking through the retreating clouds gave us one of the finest effects of the day. Every trembling leaf supported a diamond of its own, whose dazzling brilliancy put to shame the gems of royalty.

We arrived at port just as the sinking sun cast his last golden rays on the eastern hills. The black storm clouds that a few hours previous looked so threatening now lay on the distant horizon at the base of Mt. Omoa, reflecting all the bright tints of the dying day, their softened outlines melting away in the rosy haze that precedes the sudden falling of the tropical night.

From Livingston we went to Santa Thomas, having chartered a five ton sloop the "Mary Ellen," manned by three coal black sailors from Belize. We arrived one Sunday evening about eight P. M., just in time to witness the performance of some strolling acrobats from Mexico. The scene was a novel one. They had arranged their trapeze across the principal street near the wharf, in front of the cuartel or barracks, where a half dozen ragged soldiers dragged out a weary existence, and who seemed very thankful for the temporary excitement. The soldiers ran about assisting the showman in every way they could, even giving up their quarters for a dressing room, from whence the actors presently appeared, their straw colored tights embroidered with gold and silver tinsel, faces powdered and painted in the most approved style, high pointed caps and a string of small bells attached to their belts, which jingled most musically. The scene was illuminated by a row of oil lamps and the audience consisted of perhaps two hundred men, women and children. They were seated on the ground on both sides of the narrow road, the ladies with shawls over their heads smoking and laughing incessantly. The ruddy glare of the torches, the strange costumes and the babel of Indian-Spanish all combined to form a striking picture. The actors acquitted themselves in a creditable manner and must have been highly elated by the success of their performance. The crowd was good natured and not over critical, the applause frequent and prolonged, and when the perspiring comedians doffed their clown hats and made their pilgrimage through the audience they were rewarded by a shower of *reals*, each of which was acknowledged by a bow and a grimace that caused shouts of merriment.

Santa Thomas does not boast of a hotel, but we found quarters in a private house, where we were treated with the greatest courtesy, as well as to all the delicacies of the season, which consisted is this instance of the usual frijoles and tortillas with the addition of a piece of fresh pork and a cup of milk, the latter being a treat that was highly appreciated. Fruit growing is the principal industry of Santa Thomas, mostly bananas; having been requested to furnish some information on this subject, I, therefore, began to look around for facts and figures and presently found quite a lot. How much we owe to the fierce and uncompromising compiler of statistics! His bold spirit knows not fear—he seeks the depth of the tropical forest, he delves in darksome mines, climbs lofty mountains, dives

"JIM."

into the sea and measures the floor thereof—awhile he tarries in the sunny south—anon seeketh the frozen north, no height to great, no depth to vast, no region to remote—he is the hardy pioneer of human knowledge, pushing his way into the wild wilderness of undiscovered facts that hedge us about on every side. He returneth like a general at the head of an army—of figures—figures in lines, in colums, in squares, figures in companies, in regiments, in battalions, an invincible array of totals that stagger the intellect; but I feel very grateful to one of these fearless adventurers, who has given the material for the following brief chapter on bananas.

CHAPTER III.

SOMETHING ABOUT BANANAS — ARRIVE AT PUERTO CORTEZ — A TOUCH OF THE CHILLS—A MODEL HOTEL.

Although extensively cultivated along the entire coast line of Central America and the West Indies, this fruit is said to attain the highest degree of perfection along the eastern shore of Guatemala and the north coast of Honduras. This may be true, or it may be a fancy, fondly cherished by growers whose fortune it is to be located within this favored belt.

These thoughts were suggested by watching a train of mules that just passed the door, each laden with from four to six huge bunches. The reluctant animals were urged on by a half dozen Mozo's, whose dark, swarthy skin, restless black eyes and unkempt locks gave them an appearance of wild ferocity, quite out of harmony with their mild lazy dispositions. This noisy cavalcade came from a large plantation at the foot of the mountain just back of the village, from the overseer of which I have gleaned the information contained in this article.

The fruit, he informs me, is all contracted for by New York and New Orleans companies, between whom there is great rivalry, and frequently collisions occur of an ugly nature. On several occasions they have assumed so serious a character as to require the interference of the militia.

The trade has developed rapidly during the past five years and it is claimed that the importations of this year will exceed 10,000,-000 bunches, divided between New York, New Orleans, Boston, Philadelphia and Baltimore, New York taking the lead with about 3,500,000, or 140 cargoes of 25,000 bunches each. In 1830 the first full cargo of red bananas was entered at New York and consisted of 1,500 bunches, a quantity so enormous that the daring pioneer in this trade was looked upon as a "crank," harmless, perhaps, but certainly crazy.

To give a better idea of the present proportions of this industry and its rapidly increasing dimensions, I submit the following official figures giving the importations for 1887-8:

	1887—	1888—
New York	2,461,355	3,021,640
New Orleans	2,153,143	2,541,075
Boston	454,751	1,053,729
Philadelphia	315,560	1,151,938
Baltimore	529,663	280,692
	5,914,472	8,049,074

This shows a gain in one year of 2,134,602 bunches. These figures are certainly encouraging to those who contemplate opening plantations. I am told by growers here that a profit of $75 per acre can be realized with ordinary care and this, it is claimed, may be considerably increased by careful cultivation. One grower assured me that he had netted $150 per acre, but I am convinced that this was an exceptional experience. Probably a safe estimate would be $50 per acre for the first year and $60 for the next ten years. However, a net profit of $25 an acre would be better than a gold mine, without any of the risks attending such enterprises, for while the profits of fruit raising are enormous, they are at the same time very sure, for of all tropical productions, this is the one most likely to succeed with the inexperienced planter.

The banana delights in a warm, moist soil, in the neighborhood of the sea, the salt breeze being essential to its highest development. The best season for starting a "walk" or plantation, is from the middle of May to the middle of June. The bush is first cut and burned, the ground carefully cleared of all stones, weeds, etc., and the soil loosened to a depth of ten inches or a foot. The suckers are now taken from the parent stem. Strong, vigorous shoots should be selected from two to three feet high. These are cut about eight inches above the neck and placed in a slanting direction in the holes prepared for them and covered with earth, leaving only about two inches exposed. The plants mature in from 10 to 12 months, each producing a bunch of fruit averaging about 60 pounds, though specimens weighing from 90 to 100 pounds, are not rare.

There are several varieties of bananas, among which may be mentioned the red, yellow, dwarf and giant; but those most in favor in this region are known locally as the "Donbloon," "China" and "Fig." The red variety is almost entirely confined to the islands of Cuba, Jamaica and Hayti, while the yellow is most popular on the coast, and, I believe, commands the best market in the States. The dwarf is found in the interior among the mountains, often flourishing at an elevation of 5,000 feet. It is of unexcelled flavor, but to small for profitable cultivation, being only three inches in length.

The banana is not a native of America, as many suppose, but was introduced by the Spaniards shortly after the discovery of the country. By the middle of the sixteenth century it had become one of the principal food products of the newly discovered islands. It is the most nutritious of all known fruits, and forms the principal food of millions of inhabitants of tropical countries residing within thirty degrees of the equator.

The plantain is a variety of banana little known outside of the region where it produced and a small section of the Southern States, where it is highly esteemed. To the casual observer the only difference between the two products is in the size of the plant and fruit. The banana, so-called, attains a height of 18 or 20 feet, while the plaintain seldom exceeds 12 or 15 feet; but while the stalk of the the plantain is the smallest, the fruit is much the largest. The banana is usually eaten raw, while the plantain is nearly always cooked—either boiled, fried or roasted. Like the banana, the plantain does best near the sea. Its cultivation is the same, each stalk producing a single cluster of fruit. When its mission is ended its place is filled by a sucker growing from the root.

The fruit of the plantain is preserved by drying, and in some instances ground or powdered in a mortar. This product is known as "plantain meal," and is made into a number of palatable and nourishing dishes. It also produces a fine and wholesome quality of starch. It has also been utilized in the manufacture of wine, the quality of the beverage being pronounced excellent. A distillery for this purpose was established a few years ago in Honduras, but proved a failure, financially.

To give an idea of the nutritive quality of the plantain, it is asserted on good authority that a piece of ground 60 feet square will produce 4,000 pounds of fruit, which will support 50 persons two weeks, while the same space planted in wheat would not afford sustenance to more than one person for the same length of time. This explains in a large measure the lazy, shiftless habits of the natives; living in a climate with an average temperature of 80 degrees, houses are only necessary as a protection from the fierce rays of the sun or the drenching tropical rains. For this purpose four poles set in the ground surmounted by a high, pointed roof, thatched with palm leaves, answers every requirement. Clothing is not worth mentioning as the children wear none and the parents little more. With a few days work the husband can provide his family with the necessities of life for the whole year, therefore the head of the house may be seen swinging idly in a hammock, enjoying his cigarette, while his good wife prepares the meal of boiled plantains which she has just cut from the stalk that shades the hut.

A plantation once established will continue to produce for about 15 years, requiring no special cultivation other than to reap the harvest and remove the dead stalks. At the end of this time it will be found profitable to break new ground. Land suitable for this purpose can be secured at an expense of $1.00 to $5.00 per acre, according to the location. Although the fruit is maturing every month in the year, the banana season proper begins in February and continues until July; March, April, and May being the months when the business is at its best.

I am informed that a mill for grinding bananas on a large scale has recently been started at Port Limon, Costa Rica, but am unable to say what success has attended the venture which represents a considerable capital, principally from the north.

We left Santa Thomas one bright morning, arriving at Puerto Cortez just as the sun was sinking into the troubled waters of the gulf, which were now considerable agitated by a brisk breeze, that had suddenly sprung up, "just to see us into port in good style," so our dusky captain declared.

From 10 A. M. until 3 P. M. we enjoyed a dead calm, not the ghost of a zepher appeared during those five burning hours. The "Mary Ellen" lay like a log, rolling uneasily with the swell that rose and fell, with an irregular and desponding motion, as though old ocean was slowly dying, and these fitful heavings might be her last convulsive gasps. The heat was intense, the air was like the breath from a furnace, the distant shore looked like a long, pale green ribbon trembling above the water. A far-away island seemed dancing between sea and sky. The heat was fervent—that was all. We had often seen this word, often heard it repeated, but never until this day did we have any idea of its terrible meaning. The sun never appeared so close. It seemed like a great, red-hot globe that was gradually, but surely swooping down upon us. The sea, smooth as molten glass, flung back the burning air in long, wavering lines, and between the blazing sky and the simmering sea we hung, helpless, hopeless, blistering. All through these hours the captain sat at the helm, whistling a low plaintive melody or monody. It was the sailors prayer to his patron saint, San Antonia, at whose will, blows the wind, fair or ill—so our captain firmly believed: so, while the rest of us sought the slim line of shade cast by the idly flapping sail and crouched there, sweltering and envying a school of porpoises, who were playing a noisy game a few hundred yards away, or wishing we were one of those huge green turtles that now and then floated by, so calm and comfortable, independent of wind and wave. Our good captain held his place, his eyes fixed on a distant point on the horizon, which had not varried a degree for ages, it seemed to us, and whistled—very low, but very persistently—occasionally varrying the monotony by the spoken words, which we understood to be, simply a translation of the whistled tune and run something like this:

"San Antonia—San Antonia, hear a sailor's prayer,
A prayer for wind, not wild and wailing,
Just a gentle breeze, for sailing,
San Antonia—San Antonia, ruler of the air."

About three o'clock in the afternoon the sailor's patron saint seemed suddenly to become aware that someone was calling him, for about that hour the sail stretched itself once or twice, then become taut. The burnished water was broken by a thousand ripples, with here and there a tiny white cap in the distance, then more, and more, until after a little while the whole ocean seemed to be trying to run over itself, huge piles of dark green water would rise up like a wall only to come tumbling down with a crash on the heels of another roller. On we flew, grandly, gloriously, delightfully. The "Mary Ellen" was herself again, and the sailors faith in San Antonia and the magic whistle was mightily increased. So we came into port as our captain observed in "good style," just as the sun was sinking into the tumbling waters of the gulf. The houses in the distant village were touched by the golden glow that lingers but a moment after the sun disappears. We could pick out the office of the American Consular Agent, the barracks, the station, the home and office of the "Commandantee," or commanding officer, a broad low structure standing upon stilts some six or eight feet above the ground; meanwhile we were waited upon by the alcalde accompanied by a quartette of ragged soldiers, who having examined our papers and cargo, we were accorded the liberty of the port, but having heard of the clouds of mosquitoes and sand flies that rise out of the neighboring swamps about sunset, we determined to spend the night on deck and visit the town early in

"MARY ELLEN."

the morning. We, therefore, spread our blankets and stretched ourselves thereon, the air was now delightfully cool, the slight rocking of the vessel was soothing in the extreme—so, smoking and talking, we watched the lights twinkling over in the village and listened in a half dream to the music that floated out across the water from the "Hotel," where some unfortunate traveller was bravely seeking forgetfulness of the hour, by vigorously sawing on a fiddle—but at last the lights were extinguished, the unfortunate traveller either succeeded in drowning his sorrow or gave up the attempt and the only voice of the night was the low wash of the waves about the prow of the boat, as she lay gently tugging at her anchor.

We landed early in the morning and soon found our way to the only hotel, and while our practical and progressive friend looked after the commercial interests of his house, which was represented here by an agency, the writer, as the licensed idler of the party, roamed about the village seeking whom he might devour. In the course of his prowlings, he found himself in the office of the American Consular Agent at that time represented by Mr. Henry Seymour. Mr. Seymour was a bright, young fellow, a native of Grand Rapids, Michigan, and the building in which he was located was constructed in his native town and shipped to this place, a distance of about 3,000 miles and "set up" by native workmen at a cost of something less than six hundred dollars. The house consisted of three good-sized rooms with a veranda across the front; a double roof, allowing an air space of about one foot between, making the Consular office one of the coolest spots in the village, therefore, it was quite natural that we should drop in there and help our friend put in the time that appeared to drag somewhat heavily—as Consulur business seemed very quiet. Henry was quite communicative and we profited thereby, and some of the knowledge gained in those interviews will be given here, and no extra charge made. This is certainly liberal, considering the distance we had traveled to secure the information. Among other things, we made special inquiries about the healthfulness of the place. "Well," he replied, "Puerto Cortez is without doubt the healthiest point on the coast of Central America. Although a constant resident here for six years I have never known what it is to be sick—not even for a single day." This seemed remarkable and we sat a long while thinking it over, also thinking of the numerous attacks of sore throat, coughs, colds, tussels with la grippe, bilious and malarial fevers with which we had contended during the same period in a climate where the temperature varies from 70 degrees above freezing in the summer to 50 degrees below in the winter, or in other words, where we enjoy a range of 120 degrees between the extremes of heat and cold and the thermometer frequently records a variation of 20, 30, 40 and sometimes as high as 50 degrees, in less than twenty-four hours. "Here" continued Mr. Seymour, "we have an average summer temperature of 85 degrees, which, tempered as it is by the delightful sea breeze, is far from oppressive; during the dry, or winter season, the average falls to about 75 degrees, and this slight change is accomplished so gradually that the difference is not perceived, consequently there is no occasion to make any change in clothing or housekeeping arrangements on account of varying seasons. Our winters correspond with the month of June in the northern states, while our summers are cooler than the months of July and August in New York or Boston."

The prospect was charming. From where we sat we could look across the tranquil bay, beyond which, rising to the very clouds, was the dim outline of the mountains of Omoa. In the foreground a group of cocoanut trees afforded a wide patch of deep shade, where a lot of native children were playing. They were not burdened with clothes and we could not but admire the ease and freedom of their motions. The longer we gazed on this pleasant scene, the more infatuated we became. The fierce blasts of winter with their suggestive hints of coal bills, new overcoats and underwear, to say nothing of boots, scarfs, fur caps and capes for each of the children, were here unknown. Later in the day we met quite a number of old residents, persons who had become acclimated, but who, for some reason did not appear very robust, but all told the same story—"never knew what it was to be laid up" and "never sick a day," were the sterotyped phrases, and never in all our travels on that coast, were we able to find a man who had ever been ill. Threats and bribery alike failed to produce a single witness adverse to the salubrity of this wonderful climate. Men differed politically, religiously, socially; they took sides on questions of finance and government measures, and party spirit sometimes ran to bitter extremes, but on the subject of climate and health there was but one voice—Honduras possessed the finest climate in the world and the most conducive to long life and happiness. That evening we wrote a short note to our wife—the wife of our bosom—who had stood by us through many howling winters in that far north land and this was to inform her that we had found a haven of rest, but here is the letter itself:

My dear Mary Jane—I have found a perfect paradise, where sickness, sorrow and de—December are unknown, only lovely May and sweet September. It is too glorious to think about. Two bright seasons compose the blissful year, a land of beauty and plenty, where golden fruits drop at one's feet, where children need no boots—only frilled collars and straw hats, were happy mothers have nothing to do but lie in hammocks and watch the darling little creatures at their play under the spreading fronds of the cocoanut trees. Sell off everything and come at once. Excuse haste—I'm looking for a house. Will write again in a day or two."

It then occured to us that there would be no steamer leaving for the north for several days, so there was no hurry. We would leave the letter open and perhaps might be able to add that the house had been secured. Three of four days later we called again at the office of the American Consular Agency and were greatly surprised to find that gay, young representative stretched at full length on a cot—looking—well, very much like a sick man. His face was pale, his voice weak, and while his greeting was cordial it lacked the heartiness that marked our first meeting. "Look here old fellow" we said, "what's wrong? You seem to be under the weather, what has happened, lost a consignment, or a friend—surely not ill?" The consul did not reply at once, but after a moments pause, during which he lay quite still with eyes closed, he answered, but in a voice so trembling and broken that we could hardly believe it was the same that had charmed us on the occasion of our first call. "No—loss—of—business—or friend" he said, in a far away tone that was touching to hear, "and—and not—sick no—not sick." The last words seemed to cost great effort, and were accompanied by a ghastly, shivering smile that fairly rattled as it made its escape between his tightly set teeth. It was a graveyard smile—a smile that was full of horrible suggestions—it was like the fitful gleam of the sexton's lantern among the tombs at mid-night. "Not sick—no—not sick," he repeated the words feebly; and with a mournful cadence that touched our heart, but its hard to find an outlet for ones sympathy when the object of ones solicitude insists they are not ailing in the least. We suggested timidly, "Up a trifle late, or perhaps the brandy was just a wee bit strong." "No—not—that—just a touch—a touch—of—of chills—chills and—and fever—every—everybody has them—its nothing—its nothing—at—at all—please throw that—blanket—over—my—feet—there—thanks—its nothing. A dose of pills—10 grains of quinine—a couple of hours sleep—and you feel—like—a new man." This was quite a revelation to us, but we were glad to know that Henry was not sick. It is true he shook till his cot rattled half way across the room, but he did this simply because it was the custom of the country. He was perfectly well. We looked about a little more and found "everybody" had them, and had them bad. It was a part of the program and a man who refused to shake with his fellows, would be regarded as mean and selfish and would be looked upon with suspicion if not with fear. While my friend had not been "sick a day" he had lost on an average fifty days every year, or about one year out of the six. One year of freezing and burning by turns, one solid year of torture—but "never sick."

We added a postscript to our letter. "Do not make any change at present. Don't think it would pay to have a sale just now, besides there are no houses vacant at this season. While the people know nothing of sickness, they have strange shivering spells during which their teeth rattle like the "first bones" in a minstrel show, only louder and wilder. Then the oranges are not ripe and the cocoanuts often fall on the heads of the children and kill them. There are only two months in the year, but you might not like this arrangement of the calander, so please wait."

"NEVER FELT BETTER."

A few days later we began to feel that we were attracting attention—that we were being talked about. The hotel loungers would gather in little groups consulting in whispers and frequently one or another of the crowd would point over his shoulder in our direction, and from time to time some remark would be overheard, which plainly indicated that we were being discussed—and criticised severly, for in all the time we had been at the port, we had not had a chill and the natives felt that we were puffed up and proud and not inclined to be sociable. Now we did not wish to create a bad impression, and as soon as we fairly understood the sentiment of the community, we sent word around that we would have "a shake" at 3 P. M. A change occured. Everyone now seemed pleased to meet us. There was no more suspicious looks and whispered consultations. We were welcomed like a brother.

We have often thought since then that it would be almost as pleasant to be sick. The first sensation was an irresistable desire to lie down and the next a want-to-go-home feeling that was quite crushing, then a chill stole silently down our back. In a few minutes a dozen were on the field, chasing each other up and down our spinal column and taking occasional excursions down to our toes. This lasted an hour, during which we could not get enough blankets, though they were piled up about two feet high all over us. Suddenly came a change. Our head began to burn, then a flash of heat dashed in among the racing chills and for ten minutes it was a struggle which would win, but by degrees the fever gained and at last occupied the whole ground. The heat seemed unbearable. The blankets were scattered in every direction. Such racking pains in back and limbs, such bursting headache, such thirst. Finally we slept, a troubled sleep, during which we dreamed of all the cooling drinks we had ever heard. Even visions of rhe old spring house at home, with its rows of milk pans half submerged in the clear, cold water, came to torment us, but at last it was over, and as Henry had told us, we felt like a "new man," but we also felt as though we had lost several years in making the change, however, we were now acclimated and in sympathy with our townsmen and that is worth a great deal.

We always make a point of stopping at the best hotel—the best in Honduras are not usually too good. The "American" was not an exception to the rule—and this description is given free—we feel that we ought to be paid for it, but when we remember how many things we got that were not in the bill of fare, we think the least we can do is to give the "American" a free notice. It is not a very large house, and has not been painted since the Conquest of Mexico, and at the time of our visit was not crowded. By the way, it is an odd circumstance that almost every Hotel in Central America is dubbed the "American," beginning at Livingston, we find an "American House" in every town boasting a tavern, even to the capitol city. The captain of the Breakwater had described the structure so minutely that we had little difficulty in finding it, besides it had a small sign nailed up in front. We walked in but the clerk was out. The office was a small room with board partitions, on which were traced many strange names in pencil and chalk, also a few lager beer cards and some legal notices in Spanish. The ceiling was formed by stretching muslin across the joists. It must have been done a long time ago, as it was deeply stained and torn. Long shreds hung down in fanciful patterns. From various holes the cunning spider constructed his funnel shaped trap and throve mightily. The plank floor was bare, at least it would have been after a scrubbing. In one corner rested a chair with a broken leg, in another was one with a broken back, in an adjoining apartment, which seemed to be a sort of reading room, we found the third chair, a rocker, which was quite robust, with the exception of a broken arm. No one seemed to be at home, if we except a parrot, who was perched on a small table and who kept muttering morosly. We selected the strongest of the invalid chairs, and feeling that we were taking a mean advantage of one so helpless, seated ourselves as lightly as possible and awaited developments. After we had received calls from a hen and brood of chickens, a monkey and a lean hungry-looking dog, the landlady herself appeared, a creole of vast proportions. She was smoking a cigarette, but she spoke English, which was a comfort, and we soon came to an understanding. We were to have coffee at 6 A. M.; breakfast 10:30 A. M., dinner at 4:30 P. M., tea at 7 P. M., and an upstairs room, all for the very reasonable sum of $2.00 per diem. At 10:30 we appeared on the scene, but no indications of the promised meal. An interview with the landlady was not particularly satisfactory. "Bekfust soon ready," she said, and no more information was to be had. We waited—11 o'clock, 11:30, still no "signs." Meanwhile three Americans and three Spaniards had gathered in. The natives took possession of the helpless chairs and puffed away at their cigarettes quite contentedly. The Americans tramped across the room in restless rage, indulging their feelings from time to time by outbursts of language that could hardly be worked into a Sunday school oration, no matter how carefully the selection might be made. It was past 12 o'clock when a small darky appeared: "Bekfust sah," as he spoke these words he disappeared through a dark passage. We all followed and found the dining hall about such a room as the office, with a long rickety table in the center, around which the guests seated themselves and each one reached forth and helped himself. Who ever placed the breakfast on the table had vanished and we were left in undisturbed possession, being interrupted only once by the entrance of a very small girl of ebony complexion, who brought each a glass of water. At the end of the meal she came again with a pot full of black coffee.

The following extract from a letter, published in the Pittsburg Post, contains a pretty faithful description of life at the port at the time of our visit:

"In the center of the table was a large dish containing the first course, soup—bean soup. Some one had the hardihood to ladle out a portion and gently slid the dish before his left hand neighbor, on the old principle of "cut to the right and deal to the left." In this way the tureen traveled the whole length of the table. Second course, roast beef, which the same hardy pioneer started on its round in the same way. With the beef we had boiled rice, plantains, casava and frijoles, Bread, but no butter. Frijoles are simply black beans cooked down to a thick pasty mass, seasoned with salt and pepper. Casava is a root, which, when thoroughly cooked, and not to old, very much resembles our Irish potatoe, but when only half done is like so much wood. When the second course was disposed of the small colored girl appeared again, removed the plates and put in their place a cup and saucer. Then she brought a coffee-pot and a bowl of sugar. These articles made the round of the table, each one pouring out a cupful of the mixture, black and strong beyond expression. We then lit cigars and sipped the compound in true Spanish style. During the progress of the meal the chickens came in to pick up the crumbs and look after the floor in a general way, which they did very thoroughly in places. This description is not exaggerated, but rather underdrawn, every meal was a repetition. For a few days it was not so bad, but as time rolled on, it became intolerable and we formed the habit of buying canned fruits, pineapples, pickles, etc. to help out.

When evening came we asked to be shown our room. The same diminitive colored girl lit a candle and started upstairs, we followed and were more than pleased, as we had not expected such a large apartment, in fact this room included the whole second floor. We told the girl we had no use for so many cots. There were 16 scattered around, each with its little canopy of mosquito bar. Then she informed us that these cots were for the general use of the guests, and that each "gen'l'man" had an "upstairs" room. It was the only room. We felt somewhat abashed. We had never had a whole house placed at our disposal, with so many privileges before. Silently and swiftly we crept into one of the little tents; for the sandfly was there,—and his business was urgent. While we lay there thinking of all the advantages we enjoyed, a light appeared and one of the boarders quickly divested himself of his outer covering and shot under the side of the net. He did not stop to blow out the candle and we could easily see him. He was looking for something. Presently his hand came up slowly, then down with a crash. He had caught it. After a little more skirmishing around he lay down, apparently satisfied.

Nearly everyone carried gold watches, and more or less cash, but no one seemed to have any fear of robbers and took no precaution whatever. I afterwards learned that the doors were left open all night. It is but just to say that we never knew of any loss from theft, this may be owing to lack of energy on part of the native—but if you please, you may attribute it to his honesty.

In order that strangers may receive a proper impression of the dignity and strength of the Republic as a military power, it is considered necessary to have a detachment of soldiers stationed in every village. And it is well, for the impression is generally deep and lasting. At this port, which is the principal one on the Atlantic coast, there are 12 of these native warriors quartered in an old tumble-down building, known as the "Quartel." Eleven of them sleep while one leans lazily on his musket to keep them from all harm. This one is known as the "guardian angel." All are barefoot, all ragged—and not too clean. All are genuine natives, Hondurians, which means a mixture of Indian, negro and Spaniard. They are dark-skinned, with black eyes, and shocks of blach hair which hangs down over their foreheads, they are altogether without enterprise and have a hungry, hopeless look. Here they lay week after week, month after month, with no variation in their daily routine. They receive 2 reals a day (25 cents,) and out of this sum they must support themselves. The government furnishes nothing but uniforms, for which it charges a fair price—so fair, indeed, that the men have to wear a suit to tatters before they can get another. The only active duty they have to perform is at night, when the mosquitoes and sand flies come down on their defenseless quarters in blinding swarms. To make this dismal season somewhat more bearable, they light fires about the place just before sunset and cover them with green wood and grass, producing a dense smoke. In this way they spend the night in an active campaign against any invisible enemy.

By the way, I wish to state that, while these insects exist here in great numbers, they are not so large or dangerous as some writers would have you believe. I have made a special study of this subject. That the mosquitoes of Central America have been grossly and maliciously misrepresented, there can be no doubt. One writer states that "they are fully as large as a Durham cow," with "wings that spread 50 feet," that "they carry a steel-pointed bill 75 feet long," that they reach across "the street tap a man under the ear and draw all the blood out of him before he can turn around," and that the "victim falls to the ground a shriveled, corpse, so light that the winds blow him about like a dead leaf." This is all romance and should have no weight with the reader. I have examined hundreds of specimens, and have never seen one *two feet* long. They *do not* carry of children, and it is all a hoax about their boring through the thick wall of a house to reach their prey. The truth is, the very largest will not weigh five pounds, and their bills are not as long as some tailors, and not nearly so sharp. It gives me great pleasure to be able, from personal experience, to correct these misstatements of unprincipled travelers, and I would say to all who contemplate a visit to this delightful region, do not be afraid. — You can easily defend yourselves from the largest and fiercest mosquito with an ordinary "machete," or short sword, which all the natives carry for this—and other purposes.

The Country is beautiful with its cocoanut walks and orange groves and endless variety of flowering vines and shrubs. The harbor of Puerto Cortez is one of the finest on the coast, guarded by lofty mountains on the south and by a long strip of level land on the north. It is about five miles long and three wide, and so deep that the largest vessels can approach within a stones throw of the shore almost. Viewed from the sea the town presents a very pretty picture, its white houses gleaming among the deep green tropical foliage. It is also the starting point of the only railroad in the State, which makes it commercially the most important town on the coast. Banana culture is the main industry, 5000 bunches being shipped every week from this point alone. While we were at the port we witnessed the trial of a new engine or locomotive intended for the famous railroad above referred to, which connects this place with San Pedro, thirty-six miles inland. By the way, the maps show this road as completed to Amapala on the Pacific coast, but like most other Central American enterprises, this great continental line piled up a debt of $27,000,000 in the first thirty-six miles of its way, and it was thought best to stop it before it got into the mountains where it might prove unmanageable.

The locomotive refered to was not exactly new but had been made to look quite respectable by paint and polish. It was a second hand affair picked up at New Orleans by General Kraft, who practically controlled the road at this time. This was a great event. For twenty years, more or less, the natives had watched the stackless old engine drag its weary way through the one long street, and when the huge machine was placed on the track in all its glory of brass, with a huge stack and double whistle, the peo- were fairly wild, although half afraid of the monster, which now threw out smoke and sparks like a volcanoe and rushed along at the unheard of speed of 20 miles an hour. The enthusiasm was unbounded. The superintendent, sub-officers, with the alcalde and all the local great men, were seated in the tender waving their hats and bowing to the assembled multitude who answered with deafening cheers. After making three trips from the Custom House to the Lagoon, a distance of about three miles, the test was decided to be satisfactory and the machine accepted. Everybody drank to the road and its management, to the president, whose name was painted in bold characters on the pilot, to his cabinet, to the U. S. and her representatives, to everybody, and to everything.

The joy was universal, and no wonder—for years the time between the port and San Pedro had averaged ten hours and very often, owing to a breakdown, two whole days would be spent on the road—but alas! for human hopes—the test had been made on the hard road bed along the shore which owing to its proximity to the superintendent's office had been kept in pretty good condition, and it never occured to the eager purchasers to extend the trial trip to San Pedro. The first trip out, the heavy engine crushed the road into the earth and toppled over, sustaining considerable damage. Finally it was dragged back to the "lagoon" where are situated the repair shops, and where, most likely, it is lying to this day. At all events the poor old cripple that had done service for so many years was recalled, and on our last visit was still carrying freight and passengers at irregular intervals, at the very safe speed of three miles an hour."

Quite a number of Americans have recently established cocoanut plantations on this coast, and the neighboring islands, and when we consider the small capitol required, the certainty of success, and the comfortable profits, it is surprising that more have not followed their example. With proper care this thrifty palm begins to bear the fourth or fifth year from planting, and continues without intermissions for fifty years at least, just how much longer no one seems to know, though we were shown trees that were said to be seventy-five years old, that were still producing a fair quality of nuts. A "walk" once established, the proprietor may rest assured that his future is provided for, as far as income is concerned, as the demand bids fair to exceed the supply for a long time to come. Each tree in full bearing is worth from two to three dollars per annum, or from $120 to $180 per acre. The only labor required is to go over the ground at stated seasons and gather the fallen nuts into piles at convenient distances from the shore, from whence they will be taken by vessels ingaged in the fruit trade, the cash being paid as soon as the load is complete.

Cocoanuts have no season, but are constantly maturing throughout the year, on each tree will be found nuts in every stage of growth, from the blossom to those fully ripe. This tree loves the sea and flourishes best within the sound of the surf. The salt breath of the ocean is necessary to insure perfection. A Jamaica planter informed the writer that the cost of setting a grove on that island, including all expenses, until it begins to bear, will not exceed $40 per acre—what could be more delightful than a home in this land of perpetual summer, and ever blooming flowers, surrounded by the tall palms, which lay their wealth at your feet while you swing in your hammock listening to the murmur of the sea, or the melancholy paint of the musical————mosquito.

CHAPTER IV.

A CRUISE ALONG THE NORTH COAST OF HONDURAS TO TRUXILLO—LANDING IN THE BREAKERS—STUDY A WATERSPOUT—WALKER THE FILIBUSTER—SPANISH CRUELTY AND ENGLISH PERFEDY.

One day it occurred to us, that we had seen enough of Puerto Cortez. The captain of a Utilla Sloop, "The Sea Gull," of nine tons burden, happened to be on hand with an empty vessel, waiting for a commision. Having learned that he was one of the best sailors in the south, and that he was not averse to a cruise of a month, we chartered the vessel, and soon transfered our belongings to its hold, after which we bid adieu to our many friends and went aboard about 3 P. M. We rejoiced to again breathe the free air of the sea and feel the motion of the boat as it answered to the swell that was now running quite high, owing to a stiff breeze from the north, which drove the waters of the gulf through the narrow entrance of the harbor and piled them up until they splashed among the piles supporting the old store-house, which we had just abandoned and which ordinarily stood fifty feet from the shore. We lay at anchor until about sun down, when the north wind fell, and shortly after the "land" breeze came in fitful puffs, then more steadily, until our sail filled and we were under way. Our crew now consisted of Capt. Brown and mate Roland, both white, natives of Jamaica, the latter acted in the double capacity of cook and common sailor; the passengers were three in number, the writer, his cousin and colored servant, James, sometimes called Santiago. James was a native of Mexico and a bright boy of his class. He spoke the Spanish language fluently, and was well versed in the strange dialect of the Caribs, which made his services valuable in dealing with the mixed population of the coast, who invested many a shining dollar through the enticing eloquence of this dusky trader.

We stopped at a number of small villages and did a thriving trade. There are no harbors along the north coast excepting those of Puerto Cortez and Truxillo, the latter being protected on one side only, is nothing to brag of, but the towns and villages lying between those points are without harbors and landing is difficult and sometimes dangerous. Owing to the prevalence of the trade winds, there is usually a tremendous surf, and vessels are often detained several days on this account. This, of course, is a great disadvantage to these places, which otherwise are splendidly situated in the midst of the fruit belt.

We made shore at Tela, in the midst of a surf that threatened destruction to goods and passengers. Landing under such circumstances is an experience to be remembered. The Captain and Roland are good oarsmen. They are in the small boat which is being tossed about like a bubble, now it strikes the sloop with a

LANDING.

bang, the next instant is ten feet away, then back, up and down. The sloop is small and light, and rolls almost as bad as the yawl. The Captain is waiting for us to make the leap from the deck to his boat. We watch closely, the tenth part of a second too soon or too late, means a plunge into the sea. The water looks nice and cool, but a half dozen sharks have been following in our wake. They are large and hungry. We do not wish to meet them—we watch the little boat—it strikes the sloop with a crash. "Now!" shouts the captain, we leap wildly and fall in a heap, but safe. Then for the land. As we approach, the angry breakers roll higher and higher. The Captain is an expert. We ride the waves like bird, we approach the shore, the water is becoming rougher every instant, a great, green wall is piling up behind us, the captain shouts, we know he is shouting by the motion of his lips, but his words are lost—our ears are filled with the roar of the surf that is breaking along the coast for miles, it is louder than Niagara, every time we rise on the crest, of one of those green mountains we can see the shore—men are watching us—waiting for us—then we sink into a valley. For a moment nothing is visable but a streak of sky—up once more—then a shock, we have struck the sand, but fifty feet of shoal water still intervenes, men rush out to meet us—they motion us to jump on their backs. Our cousin is a light weight. He leaps nimbly on the shoulders of a stalwart native and is borne safely to the land. The captain, Roland and James all go safely. I hesitate, having never been carried since I can remember—don't like the idea—native looks weak—no other way. Indian says "come," only word of English he knows. I go, he trembles under me—will he reach the shore? He hesitates, then, with a snort like a wild horse he staggers forward. I pity him, offer to get down and help, but he don't understand and before I can make my meaning clear, he is on land. "Kiramba," is the only word he utters as he falls on the sand, sprawling at full length. Thus we land at Tela, a village of huts, with a few orange trees and cocoanut palms and some small banana plantations. A few soldiers, one of whom died during our visit and we saw him buried with scant ceremony in his ragged uniform, and without a coffin.

Two incidents occured during our stay in this village, that serve to fix the place indelibly in our minds. The first was the passing of a waterspout and as it was the first event of the kind we ever witnessed, we were much impressed by the spectacle. The following account is taken from the Pittsburg Post:

"About three o'clock this afternoon, while enjoying our usual siesta, we were aroused by a strange noise—it was unlike anything I had heard, and I listened for a minute or so, trying to account for it without the trouble of getting up, for as yet I was only half awake. The air was heavy and close, as though charged with some noxious gas; breathing required an effort that was unnatural. We seemed to be under the shadow of some uncertain peril. The interior of the grove was dark as a deserted church.

Meanwhile the mysterious din increased to a heavy rumbling roar, to which were now added a variety of notes, sharp, shrill, hissing, at times so piercing as to amount to a shriek, almost human in its intensity. There was also a succession of sharp reports with a crackling sound like that produced by the burning of a cane brake.

Now fully awake I tumbled from my hammock in haste, and sought the source of all this commotion. Emerging from the deep shadows of the grove I was confronted by the most remarkable spectacle I had ever witnessed. Within a quarter of a mile of the shore a gigantic waterspout was moving slowly in a westerly dir-

A WATERSPOUT.

ection almost parallel with the line of breakers that lashed the coast. At this distance the appearance was peculiar and striking. A dark column rose from the water to the cloud above, which seemed torn by contending winds, so that great sections of the black curtain were every moment whipped off and went tumbling downward only to be drawn within the terrible vortex and again sent skyward and there scattered in a thousand fragments by the opposing forces above. Thus there was a constant downward rush of clouds at a short distance from the center of action, and a constant upward rush close to the rising column as they were drawn within the influence of the whirlwind.

At the base of the pillar, which grew heavier and blacker every moment, the water was lashed into a state of fury quite indescribable. Clouds of spray obscured the sea for a distance of one hundred yards or more, beyond which it was comparitively smooth. Although frequent and vivid flashes of lightning played among the writhing masses of vapor, there was no following crash of thunder, which struck one as remarkable at the time, though I am now convinced that the sound was simply drowned, as it were, by the superior roar of wind and waves. The scene presented was grand and fearful. The heavy brow of the approaching cloud bulged downward as though ready to burst with the accumulated weight of water; the color of this advance guard was a dull olive, almost black, merging into a sulphurous yellow on the edges of the heavy folds, among which the lurid flashes gleamed incessantly. It seemed like a hand-to-hand conflict between the forces of air and water, and we watched it with intense interest, and some apprehension, for several minutes, after which the wind seemed to have spent its strength, the stately shaft began to waver and soon broke near the center, the upper portion mingling with the clouds, the lower part falling back into the sea which soon became calm as the surrounding surface.

Three minutes later the over-burdened clouds, unable longer to support the tremendous weight imposed on them, gave way, and the downpour that followed baffles description. It was not rain in the ordinary sense; the water did not fall in drops, but in streams, producing a fine spray that hid all but the nearest objects. Although our house was situated on a high knoll it trembled under the pressure, and we seemed surrounded by the sea. Fortunately this did not last but a few seconds, else the very earth must have been washed away. As it was, the lower portion of the village was inundated and many houses destroyed.

I have described in a feeble way the appearance of what is

popularly known as a waterspout, but which is nothing more or less than a whirlwind of unusual violence, occuring on the water instead of land, and gathering up in its strong arms the spray from the waves, in place of dust, leaves and other light material encountered when traversing the same distance over fields and woods.

The primary cause of whirlwinds has never been satisfactorally explained. The commonly accepted theory is, that they are produced by the action of counter currents of air, that is, two currents, moving in opposite directions meet and instead of sliding along smoothly and peaceably, as they should, one will try to induce the other to change its course, which the other naturally refuses to do, the consequence is, a portion of air from either side becomes engaged in a violent tussel pulled to the right on one hand, to the left on the other, until in the confusion it forgets which side it belongs to, and gaining in strength, declares itself an independent body, and goes whirling along quite indifferent to all the laws of air, a windy rebel, full of blow and bluster!

The only plausible, I should say reasonable, theory that has been advanced was given a few years ago by a writer who said the atmosphere surrounding the earth might be compared to a series of blankets, stretched one above the other, the dividing line usually being marked by clouds of various forms arranged in horizontal lines, their character varying according to their height. On certain occasions a stratum of very warm air lies immediately over the earth's surface, right above this we find a second stratum of cold air. The hot air being light presses upward with a constant effort to escape, but is held in place by an equally firm pressure from above, but it sometimes happens that the overlying blanket has been worn thin in places and the hot air taking advantage of the situation rips out a square and rushes through. News of the breach spreads rapidly, and soon all the warm air in the vicinity hurries forward watching for an opportunity to crowd out into the cool space above. My authority goes on to say that the motion of the air near this opening is precisely the same as that produced in a basin of water by suddenly removing the stopper in the bottom. The rapid displacement of the lower portion causes a commotion which in a second or two extends to the surface, forming a minature whirlpool which continues to revolve until all the water has escaped.

The accompanying illustration, from a sketch made on the spot, will give the reader some idea of a waterspout as viewed by the writer from a distance of one-fourth of a mile, or there about. Two miles out the sun is brighthly shining and the tiny white caps flash merrily. Far away, on the horizon, a couple of schooners bound for some southern port, are tranquiling sailing, apparently unconscious of their dangerous neighbor; but the captains have already noted the storm and carefully computed its distance, its speed and direction. They knew long ago that there was nothing to fear from this revolution of the winds."

The other event which renders Tela quite unforgetable was the result of a trait peculiar to the native. While the experience was purely personal, its rehearsal will serve as an illustration of Honduriau character and for this purpose we again quote from the "Post."

"The politeness of the Spaniards is proverbial. Sometimes it is excessive—I might say oppressive. They place their houses, furniture and servants at your disposal. Do you contemplate a journey, they will furnish horses as well as Mozos, and accompany you in person quite regardless of the sacrifice to their own interests. If you admire an article you are at once informed that "it is yours." Yesterday my traveling companion, himself a man of family and a lover of children, stopped at a wayside cottage in quest of bananas. He says he was met in the doorway by a baby of the brunette type, a dark, rich, walnut color, with a shock of black tangled hair and great fishy, staring eyes. It was naked. With one dusky hand resting on the bamboo frame it aided its faltering steps, with the other it grasped a large piece of "dulce" (native sugar,) which it sucked with evident satisfaction. Wishing to make a good impression at the start, and well knowing a mother's weakest point, he began to extol the infant's charms in the warmest terms. Such lovely eyes! Such a heavenly complexion! Such a sweet expression! (literally true.) He says he will never forget the feeling of amazement, followed by one of horror and disgust, when the polite senora thrust the squirming youngster into his arms saying, "take him, he is yours.' I do not wish to question my friends veracity—but this sounds like a—well say a chestnut re-roasted.

I had been suffering silently several days from a defective

tooth. One morning the pain was so great I could not conceal my annoyance. It was a large, double molar, wayback in the upper jaw. I was almost frantic. There was no dentist within a hundred miles. Our good host, Don Jose, noticing my agitation, inquired the cause and at once offered his services. His father had practiced dentistry years ago, and among the old heirlooms was a pair of forceps of ancient pattern. They were covered with a thick coating of rust—dark red—horribly suggestive. For a half hour I had been seriously contemplating self-destruction, but the moment my importunate friend appeared with this frightful instrument of emancipation the pain ceased, and life seemed a sweet and priceless possession.

I hastened to assure him of my recovery and begged him not to trouble himself further, adding, that I should always feel under obligations for the unselfish interest manifested in my behalf. But he was not to be moved. The tooth should be taken out by all means. It would not be any trouble, on the contrary he would consider it a personal favor to be allowed to "serve senor." It would be a mark of respect and confidence that would be appreciated and treasured in his memory for years, he said. Meanwhile a crowd of natives had gathered about the door. His wife and daughter came in and added their entreaties to those of the ardent Don. The spectators were becoming restless. Murmurs of impatience were heard. Insinuations, muttered half aloud, reached my ears. Some of these were not exactly flattering to my vanity. 'Bockra man too much 'fraid.' This was more than my pride could bear. I offered myself an unwilling and trembling sacrifice to that man's vain ambition. Oh!

From Tela we went to Ceiba, where we were landed in the usual picturesque fashion. This pretty little city nestles at the foot of Conger Hoy, the highest mountain in Honduras. It has a population of about 4000. Being situated in the center of the banana belt, it enjoys a degree of prosperity unequaled by any town on the north coast. It is well built of frame and adobe houses, many of them neatly painted, their red-tiled roofs gleaming among banana and cocoanut "walks," which abound on every side. I am told that the shipments of bananas from this point alone average about 100,000 bunches monthly during the busy season, which includes April, May, June and July.

The thunder of the surf makes endless music for the lover of nature, but the contending waves interfere sadly with the work of loading vessels which have to anchor about a mile away beyond the line of breakers. All fruit must be taken out in lighters, and the difficulty of "putting off" and landing in these raging waters can only be appreciated by those who have enjoyed the personal experience. Often the sea is so rough that even the Caribs, who are expert sailors, are unable to launch a boat. At such times I have known steamers to lie nearly a week waiting for the angry waters to subside.

The scenery in this vicinity is charming. The lofty dome-like crest of Conger Hoy rises to a height of 8,040 feet, clothed with verdure to its very top. This is an extinct volcano, and the shore is strewn with pumice stone thrown from its crater centuries ago, for it has not been active since the discovery of America. Sometimes in the early morning a beautiful and startling effect is produced. The base, shrouded in mist, seems far away, dim and indistinct, while the summit, towering far above the clouds, every projecting rock and shadowy ravine revealed by the slanting rays of the rising sun, seems thrust forward until it overhangs the town. So striking is this illusion at times that one can hardly resist the feeling of awe, almost of fear, inspired by the strange spectacle.

MOUNT BONITA.

To the westward stands the twin peak of Bonita, almost as high and much more precipitous. The two are connected by a series of lofty ridges, presenting in places an unbroken rock wall 2,000 feet high. It is only by comparison that the mind can grasp comprehensively such tremendous elevations. To do so, stand before the Masonic Temple (Chicago,) on the Soldiers monument (Indianapolis,) look up to the top of the shaft, measure well the distance, then, if your imagination is strong enough, pile six towers of the same height on the one before you. This will will give some idea of the precipice presented by the huge ragged spur that connects these giants.

These are the mountains that guided the storm-tossed vessels of Columbus when on his fourth voyage he vainly sought for a strait through which he might sail into the undiscovered seas to the westward. It was within a few leagues of this place that he landed on the 14th day of August, 1502, to attend mass, which was celebrated under the trees, in the presence of the sailors and a large number of natives, who had assembled for the double purpose of satisfying their curiosity and bartering the products of the country for European trinkets.

And here we are to-day trading with the decendants of these same natives in much the same manner, transporting our stock on mules, traveling for days through unbroken forests, traversing dense jungles or toiling wearily over mountains. Four centuries, so eventful in other parts of the earth, seem to have left no impression on this land of hammocks and dreamy repose." One evening we found ourselves before the ancient city of Truxillo.

In the year 1524 or 1525, Hernando Cortez, then in the zenith of his fame, arrived at this port, which was at that early date, a place of considerable importance. Cortez had left the capital of Mexico for the express purpose of punishing the rebel Christoval de Olid, a brave but unprincipeled general, whom the ruler of New Spain had instructed to establish a settlement on the north coast of Honduras, and to that end he was intrusted with a small army to carry out the enterprise, which, having accomplished, he decided to set up a government of his own. However, the story of his disaffection finally reached the ears of the Vice Roy, who at once despatched a faithful follower, Francisco de las Casas, with orders to arrest the rebel—but the avenger fell into the hands of Olid and was made a prisoner, but after a time was released. No sooner was he at liberty than he began plotting the overthrow of

Olid and at last succeeded in securing enough followers to carry out his purpose, and Christoval de Olid was promptly beheaded. Meanwhile Las Casas, having remained absent so long, Cortez fearing that he had been overtaken by some disaster, decided to go to his rescue and at the same time punish his rebellious general in such a way that the example would be an object lesson to others who might be tempted in the same manner. Cortez finding his mission fulfilled, so far as Olid was concerned, spent some time exploring the country near the mouth of the Rio Dulce, after which he fitted up two brigantines and continued the expedition with a view of exploring more thoroughly the coast of Honduras. It was during this excursion that he visited the port now known as Truxillo or Trujillo, as the Spaniards frequently write it. The surf was running so high that he decided not to land, but the inhabitants "were so overjoyed that they rushed into the shallow water and eagerly bore the general in their arms to the shore." Just so, we have been carried at almost every place on the coast and our heart swells with pride to think that our appearance has been hailed with almost the same enthusiasm that greeted the renowned Cortez, and that people have splashed out through the salt water for the purpose of carrying us ashore, for pure love and admiration—of our pocket book.

OLD FORT TRUXILLO.

The city possesses a fair harbor, being partly sheltered by a long narrow strip of land, which runs out to the east of the town, and as the prevailing winds are from that direction, landing ordinarily is easily accomplished. We arrived at this place on the 15th of July. The sea being calm, we went on shore at once. The principal part of the town is built on a narrow plateau about eighty feet above the sea, but the custom house and a few wholesale stores are clustered about the landing and along the line of the street leading up to the main portion of the city. This road is cobbled from wall to wall and is very long and steep and those who have walked its length under the tropical sun, will not soon forget the tramp, but at the end we are rewarded by the sight of the "Posado Crespo," one of the finest, best equipped and managed hotels in Honduras. Here we were alloted rooms on the second floor, large, airy apartments opening on a long balcony overlooking the plaza.

The plateau on which the city is built is perhaps a half mile wide, immediately back of which the mountains rise to the clouds. Like most towns on the coast, the Caribs represent the working class and we took advantage of the opportunity to secure a sup. ply of pine apples. This matchless product of the tropics here attains its highest degree of perfection, its cultivation requiring only the slightest effort, yet with all these advantages, and in face of the fact that it always commands a good market, the indolent natives refuse to take the trouble to raise it, hence our appreciation of the industrious habits of the caribs, whose enterprise made it possible for us to enjoy this delicious fruit to the fullest extent.

Truxillo or Trujillo, was founded sometime previous to 1525, probably about 1520, for it was an established settlement enjoying a considerable trade at the time of the visit of Cortez. While this famous general was being feasted in the village and his brigantines were rocking idly in the sunny sea, John de Verrazano was exploring the cold and cheerless shores of New York, but it was almost a hundred years later that the first permanent settlement was made by the Dutch on Manhattan Island, thus it will be seen that Truxillo is one of the oldest towns in America being from 30 to 40 years older than St. Augustine, Fla.

Among the interesting specimens of ancient Spanish architecture, the old church and ruined fort will probably have the greatest attraction for the visitor, especially if he has a taste for antiquities. The crumbling towers of the old fortification with its walls covered with vines, forms one of the most picturesque objects in the town, and if the tourist is artistically inclined he will not leave without carrying with him some sketches of this romantic ruin. The modern town is built of adobe and many of the houses were neatly painted and quite a number of new structures were under course of construction.

We were not long in learning that Truxillo was even more healthful than Puerto Cortez, and fever was quite unknown but a many persons had the same strange spells of shivering that were noted at all other points on the coast, and during our short stay there were several deaths. Among those who were "never sick" was a young man from New York. He was quite delirious and talked incessantly about the cool spring on his father's farm, which was situated near Albany. In any other country this man would have been considered "quite under the weather," but not so here. "He'll be up in a day or two" said the doctor, and the doctor was right, two days later found him "up" on the hill, but he did go of his own volition. If this case had occured in one of our own ports, it would have been classed yellow fever and the town quarantined; but they have no such troubles in this happy land. The deception so universally practiced by the officials, and in some cases by the leading merchants and planters in regard to the prevalence of deadly fevers is nothing short

BREAD TREE AND FRUIT.

of criminal, and is altogether inexcusable, as by taking such wise precautions as have been noted in the more progressive town of Belize, the ravages of this dread disease (call it yellow fever or black, as you prefer, its equally fatal) would be greatly diminished if not wholly avoided.

This reckless indifference to the welfare of visitors and possible investors, the outgrowth of selfishness and ignorance, satisfactorily accounts for the backward conditions of society and trade along this coast which under happier circumstances might enjoy a high degree of prosperity. It was at this place that Wm. Walker of Filibuster fame met his death. Those unfamiliar with the history of this famous outlaw will find an admirable account of his life and wild raids in the book entitled "Story of the Filibusters," by James Jeffrey Roche, to which we are indebted for the following record of his sentence and death. "To capture the town of Trujillo on the mainland was but work of half an hour, only a few of the assailants being wounded. Walker received a slight wound in the face. Scarcely had the town been occupied when a British war steamer, the Icarus, appeared on the scene. Captain Salmon, her commander, immediately notified Walker that the British Government held a mortgage against the revenues of the port as security for certain claims, and that he intended to protect the interests of his government by taking possession of the town. Walker replied that he had made Trujillo a free port and consequently could not entertain any claims for revenues which no longer existed. The captain refused to recognize any change in the government of Honduras and sent a peremptory demand for surrender, promising in case of compliance to carry the prisoners back to the United States, and threatening to open fire on the town if his demand was not immediatly complied with, meanwhile General Alverez with 700 soldiers was preparing to make an assualt by land, thus hemmed in Walker determined to evacuate Trujillo, which he did the following night retreating down the coast with only seventy men. In their haste they were compelled to leave behind all their heavy baggage and accoutrements, carrying only thirty rounds of ammunition each, the rest they destroyed. When the British landed next morning they were only in time to protect the sick and wounded in the hospital from the ferocious Hondurians. The Icarus immediately took Alvarez and a strong force on board and steamed down the coast in pursuit. At the mouth of the Rio Negro they learned that Walker lay encamped at the Indian villiage of Lemas whither the boats of the Icarus were sent. They found the adventurers in no condition to oppose such overwhelming odds. They carried with them only two barrels of bread and being without blankets or overcoats many had been attacked with fever from sleeping on the damp ground. To Captain Salmon's demand for unconditional surrender, Walker replied with the inquiry whether he was surrendering to the British or Hondurians? Captain Salmon twice assured him distinctly and specifically that it was to her Majesty's forces, whereupon the Filibusters laid down their arms and were carried on board the Icarus. On arriving at Trujillo, Captain Salmon, turned his prisoners over to the Hondurian authorities despite their protest and demand for trial before a British tribunal. Walker was arraigned before a court-martiel on the eleventh of September and after a brief examination was condemned to die by the fusillade next morning. He heard his sentence with calmness and was remanded to prison to pass the night in preparing for death. At half past seven o'clock on the morning of September 12th he was led out to the place of execution. He walked unfettered with a calm firm tread. He carried the crucifix in his left hand, a hat in his right. A priest walked by his side reciting prayers for the dying. Two soldiers walked before him carrying drawn sabres, three more followed him with bayonets at the charged.

THE DENTIST.

Upon entering the hollow square of soldiery on the plaza, he begged the priest to ask pardon in his name of anyone whom he had wronged in his last expedition, then mounting the fatal stool he addressed his executioners in Spanish, as follows:

"I am a Roman Catholic. The war which I made in accordance with the suggestion of some of the people Ruatan was unjust. I ask pardon of the people. I receive death with resignation, would that it might be for the good of society," Then calm as he had ever been in peace or in war, he awaited the fatal signal. The captain of the firing party gave a sharp order, dropped the point of his saber and at this sign three soldiers stepped forward to within twenty feet of the condemned man and fired their muskets. All of the balls took effect but still the victim was not dead, whereupon a fourth soldier advanced, and placing the muzzle of his piece to the forehead of the victim, blew out his brains—and so died the last of the Filibusters."

Though Walker, the outlaw, freebooter and usurper, may have richly deserved the fate which overtook him in the plaza of this ancient town, language cannot frame a sentence bitter enough to properly express the feeling of scorn which is aroused in recalling the perfidy of Captain Salmon, whose treachery in thus delivering his prisoners into the hands of his enemies, after faithfully promising to carry him and his wretched companions to the United States, could only be matched by the brutal and inhuman savages into whose hands he played. It seemes incredible that an English officer of his rank and intelligence could have been guilty of such baseness. I hope my readers will not attribute this outbreak to sectional feeling or national antipathy—it was simply a case of individual barbarity and for fear these words may be misconstrued as aimed at the British as a class, I will recite another incident which goes to show that the English heart is not always on the wrong side. The story is told in the following letter, recently printed in the "News."

"Now that the brief misunderstanding between this courtry and Great Britain is happily at an end, and we are shaking hands and congratulating each other on the peaceful settlement of the difficulty, it is pleasant to recall an incident in which her majesty's armed sloop Niobe once did us a friendly turn. It was during the Cuban Rebellion of 1868-76 and the date was November, 1873. A vessel, the Virginus, sailing under the United Sates flag had been captured by the Spanish gunboat, Tornado, and carried into the harbor of Santiago, where here crew and over 100 passengers were thrown into prison. Among the latter were four insurgent leaders, Senores Ryan, Cespedes, Varona and Del Sol. These were immediately tried by the Spanish Military Court and five days after the capture were shot, their heads cut off and carried about the streets on pikes, while some of the bearers pressed the ghastly relics against the bars of the prison windows, as a reminder of the fate the captives might expect. Having so quickly dispatched these rebels, the thirst for blood was increased ten fold. The remaining prisoners were at once treated to a mock trial and condemned to death. No attention was paid to the protests of the English and American Consuls and on the seventh day of November, Captain Fry an American citizen, and fifty-one companions were cruelly butchered in the presence of a howling mob, who were allowed to mutilate the dead bodies as they choose. This fiendish work was not only permitted but was encouraged by the Spanish commander. It seems incredible that such atrocities could have been perpetrated in the present century by a Christian nation, but such are the facts which are well authenticated. About ninety poor wretches still remained in confinement, and in spite of the earnest protest of our representatives supplemented by the efforts of the English Consul, the entire number where condemned to death and the hour set for their execution. No American vessel was in those waters at that time, but thanks to the ever present English man of war the armed sloop Niobe lay at Kingston within a days sail. No sooner had her commander, Sir Lambton Lorraine, heard of the work going on at Santiago than he set sail for that port, where he arrived promptly and without waiting for instructions or consulting anyone, he at once demanded the reprieve of the condemned men, most of whom were Americans, and when General Burriel sought to argue the question, he quickly brought the debate to a close. You have murdered British subjects, he declared, and are holding others in prison, release them immediately or I will blow your town to atoms! There was no dallying, the Niobe's ports were open, her guns trained and every man at his post. It required only a signal from the commander to bring down a storm of shot and shell that would soon have reduced the town to a mass of smoking ruins. Burriel made one more effort by insisting that only Americans were concerned, thinking by this assertion to arouse the prejudice of the English commander. The ruse did not succeed. If that is the case, replied Lorraine, I will take the responsibility of protecting American citizens, if you do not at once comply with my demands I will open fire. The Spaniard was forced to accept the terms and to this friendly but unwarranted act of an English captain, nearly a hundred lives were saved, a large proportion of whom were citizens of the United States. Possibly the Englishman erred in a diplomatic point of view by taking the high-handed course adopted on this occasion, but we cannot help admiring the courage that moved him to act so promptly and vigorously in behalf of the little band of Americans who would have been shot like dogs within a few hours. The episode furnishes one example at least when a British man of war was a welcome sight to Yankee eyes, and the remembrance at this time cannot fail to hasten the return of an era of good felling on the part of the two great powers, that after all are very closely allied in all that appeals to the great heart of humanity.

ANCIENT GATE TRUXILLO.

CHAPTER V.

VISIT THE BAY ISLANDS, BONACCA, RUATAN, UTILLA—A NIGHT OF STORM—BACK AT THE PORT.

From Truxillo we returned to Puerto Cortez by way of the Bay Islands, visiting Bonacca, Ruatan and Utilla in succession. This part of the trip was like a holiday excursion and will always be remembered with pleasure. The first day's sail was rather rough owing to headwinds which kepts us on the "tack" during the whole day and the motto of the hour was, "Look out for the boom," for with each change of course the heavy timber would swing across the deck with teriffic force, and fearfully close to the floor, so whenever we heard the warning cry all hands fell flat. The waves were glorious and we could not sufficiently admire the beautiful play of color as the light penetrated the rising crest that fell a moment later in a sheet of glistening foam. The breeze continued fresh, flocks of gulls wheeled about over head while vast schools of porpoises churned the sea into a creamy foam. Occasionally a wave of unusual dimensions would sweep the deck drenching us to the skin in spite of our huge oil skin coats or "slickers," which we had provided for such emergencies, but with a temperature averaging about 85 degrees, a ducking was not such a disagreeable experience. Here and there some pirate of the deep, would be be seen in pursuit of its legitimate prey, the flying fish, but apparently meeting with small success, the little fellows being to quick for them; as they rose from the water in the distance they looked like flakes of burnished silver floating in the air—their flight was swift and extended from one hundred to two hundred yards, at a time. One struck the sail and fell on deck, which we captured, but soon restored to liberty and the chances of being devoured by its old enemy.

Bonacca is a picturesque little island, inhabited by a mixed population of Indians, negroes and half breeds and one or two whites. Like all other places on the coast, this town was noted for its healthfulness—indeed, the climate was so excessively salubrious the inhabitants could not live on the mainland but built their village a mile or more from shore, where a coral reef formed the foundation for the miserable huts which were raised on piles about four feet above the water. All communication was carried on in boats. As might be expected under such circumstannces, the citizens of this western Venice are lawless and ignorant, their principal diversion being found in cutting each others throats. The only incident recalled at this place occured on the evening of our arrival. A couple of Indians had been indulging their tastes for carnage, by hacking each other heads with their ever ready machetes- As is usual in such affrays, one of the pair was killed. The "Comandante" sent a couple of half clad soldiers to arrest the criminal. They succeeded in capturing him and were proceeding to the Cabildo in their boat, when the prisoner, succeeding in freeing his hands, made a sudden leap for liberty. He swam with the greatest ease but the soldiers followed him closely belaboring him with their oars until he sank from exhaustion. He was then dragged out and carried to headquarters in an insensible condition, covered with blood. The scene was revolting and we were glad to leave the miserable island, which under a stable and civilized goverment might be made one of the pleasantest resorts in the south.

From Bonacca to Ruatan is some 30 or 40 miles, the wind being favorable the "sea-gull" fairly leaped from wave to wave. We were now in the track of the trade winds which blow with such regularity that they cause a surface current that bears the boat along as on a river. The same wind carried Columbus and his intrepid followers gaily along the same path four hundred years before, but proved a perfect demon when he attempted to return and he was forced to "tack" along the shore of the main land, much as we had done on our outward journey, but we were in the "swim" now and a few hours sailing found us at the little harbor of Oakridge, Island of Ruatan. The entrance to this pretty little bay is scarcely wide enough to admit a vessel being protected by a long line of coral reefs. A couple of poles firmly fixed in an upright position indicated the exact location of the opening and by carefully maneuvering, our captain steered the sloop safely between the rocks over which the water was roaring with a voice louder than thunder. We only stopped at this place long enough to secure a fresh supply of water and pineapples, and to call on some English boat builders, the Cooper Bros., who, with their parents had made this lonely, but lovely harbor their home for many years.

Here we saw the bread fruit, and the tree which produces it. We were dissapointed—instead of nice crisp, brown leaves hanging from every limb ready for the table, we found only a green spongy sort of substance about the size of a cauliflower, which it somewhat resembles; it was not good raw, and was worse boiled, but it is said to be nutritious; it will sustain life, which is about all the natives care for; however, if the fruit is not quite up to ones expectations the tree itself surpasses them. It is beautitul and attains huge proportions, and should be cultivated for shade and ornament if for nothing else, its wide spreading branches and light green foliage, which forms an agreeable contrast to the denser growths, making it particularly desirable for public highways or private grounds. From here we went to Coxenhole, the largest town on the island but were prevented from landing by reports of yellow fever, which some evil minded person had circulated but which, of course, were indignantly denied by the Spanish officials. However, the American Consul, Mr. Burchard, came abroad our vessel and advised us to stay on the boat, for, said he, "while there may be no fever in the town, quite a number of persons have persisted in dying every day and almost without warning. Two of my office force have been carried 'up the hill' within the last forty-eight hours." Neither had been "sick," they simply died, to be in fashion perhaps, but as we had no ambition to keep up with the style and cared very little for the opinions of these people, we decided to run the risk of incurring their displeasure by continuing in this vulgar state of existence; so after viewing this interesting old town for a few hours from the deck of the sloop and taking on a supply of fresh water and fruit, we put about and were soon in the open, flying before the trade wind that had favored us ever since leaving Bonacca. The sea was glorious, the sky a peculiarly deep blue flecked here and there with light feathery clouds that took many fantastic forms. Refering to my note book for that date, I find the following: "Good breeze—heavy sea—captain says we are making nine knots—pretty fair—throw out line—catch a Barracuda—gamy fish—showed fight—weight, 15 pounds—Roland prepares same for dinner, not all, only part—elegant—throw out again, man on lookout shouts "a whale"—everybody makes a dash for the line; find it very hot, drop it—James fingers cut to the bone—a royal battle; we get oakum to protect hands, all sieze line, but with our united efforts cannot pull him up, he thrashes the water like a whirlwind, then down, the length of the line, he is huge—but is growing weaker after a half hour tug we haul him in, not a whale—a dolphin—beautiful fish."

Having read so much concerning the changing colors that play over the surface of the dolphin while dying, I took particular pains to ascertain if the published accounts were really true, as I had always been somewhat skeptical on the subject. I draw on my note book again. "The fish when first landed was a bright golden yellow, with brilliant green spots. In less than five minutes the yellow, which formed the back ground, changed to a bright green and the spots to a vivid blue. For the next three minutes scarcely any change occured. Then the green became almost

YOUNG COCOANUT PALM, FOURTH YEAR FROM PLANTING.

white, the blue spots continuing the same. A little later the white suddenly became a deep bronze green, the spots a brilliant yellow with a touch of carmine and the whole surface took on a peculiar metalic lustre. These shades continued with little change until the fish was quite dead." The effect was striking and with very little aid of the imagination, the poet's conception would be fully realized.

Nothing could be more delightful than this trip. The air was cool but never chilly, the ever changing panorama of mountain and sea, the ceaseless music of the surf as it broke over the coral reefs that everywhere guard the coast like a line of pickets—all restraints of civilization were for the time cast aside, we reveled in our freedom like boys just out of school. We lolled about the deck, and read or dozed, or fished or listened to Roland's wild songs. The play of the awkward porpoises was a constant source of amusement. These huge black fish seem to have nothing in the world to do but race about in schools of a dozen or more, chasing each other like children at play, frequently leaping out of the water and coming down like an avalanche, lashing the sea into a white froth. Often we sat up late at night watching the phosphorescent glow of the waves or the ever shifting lines of light reflected from the moon, which shone with a brilliancy unknown in the north.

We varied the monotony by a daily bath on the deck, or in the surf along shore. We enloyed the most extraordinary appetites. Roland declared, three more such passengers would be worse than a visitation of locusts. Our meals were served on tin pans and our coffee in tin cups, the only kind of ware that could live through the buffetting our little vessel endured, but a hungry traveler cares little for the ways of society, or its fancy dishes, and I am sure men never enjoyed their meals better than we. The Fifth Avenue with its elaborate menu and elegant service never awakened the keen zest with which we attacked our beans and bacon. Referring again to my notes, I find: "July 19th, have just finished dinner—fish (baracuda) caught about an hour ago, roasted plantains, casava, bread, tinned butter, Holland corned beef, beans, bananas, pineapples, coffee, milk in tins from France, cigars from Cuba."

After dinner we smoked and read, exchanged yarns, landed another fish. Just as the sun was sinking between the island mountains. the captain, by a skillful maneuver, turned the "gull" into the harbor or Utilla. This is an English settlement and has an air of thrift and purpose that is usually lacking in the Spanish towns. Having ascertained that there was nothing to be feared, from fever at this place, we were soon on snore. This was the home of the captain and Roland, and at their request we decided to stop here a day or two and make some sketches along the coast, which is very wild and picturesque. The village is small and of little importance as a trading point. Some bananas and pineapples were shipped from this place. While here we were entertained by Mr. Rose, the principal merchant of the port. His home the most modern in the village, attested the good tas'e of its inmates, consisting of Mrs. Rose and her two handsome daughters. It had been so long since we had entered a house provided with carpets and modern furniture, we hardly knew how to behave. Since leaving Belize three months ago, we had not found a building containing any of these luxuries, with the single exception of the hotel at Truxillo. Here we found not only carpets, but papered walls hung with pictures, upholstered chairs, carved tables, a piano, bedsteads of the latest pattern with springs and white sheets. It semed like a veritable palace to us, and then the fresh bread and real butter, the snowy cloth, the china, the tea and toast, the well trained servant who glided noislessy about, always appearing just when wanted, and vanishing at the proper moment; the hearty good will of the parents, the ready wit, and merry laughter of the young iadies, all combined to make our day at Utilla one to be remembered with pleasure. But like all earthly pleasures, this came to an end, and bidding our friends good bye, we returned to the deck of the boat which somehow seemed to have lost much of its attractiveness during our brief absence. Although the sky looked threatening, our captain decided to start about four o'clock. Roland protested stoutly. He was sure a storm was brewing, and he thought no harm could come of tarrying a few hours longer, but the captain was not to be moved. He declared he could weather any gale that was likely to arise and as we were all anxious to get back to the Porte, where a week or two must be consumed in preparations for the over land trip, we took sides with the skipper. the air was heavy, a strange, dull gray mist hung over the distant mountains, the surf, breaking on the reefs a couple of miles southward moaned in a most melancholy way, the coral caverns along the shore seemed to catch and muffle the sound of the swirling water. The sea birds shrieked ominously, the gulls flew low, a brass colored sun glimmored faintly through a murky haze, but the captain laughed at the fears of his mate, and at the appointed hour we were on board, picking our way slowly among the fishing vessels that crowded the little harbor. About five P. M. we found ourselves clear, the breeze was fresh and as the sun neared the horizon the haze became thicker, until from a sickly yellow, the great ball turned to a dull red, tinging the whole sky with a firey glow. This was reflected by the water which now took the hue of molten copper. The distant peak of Conger Hoy was covered by a dark mass of clouds, whose black folds, slowly envelloped his giant shoulders gradually blotting out ravine or rocky precipice; from the midst of the writhing vapors, The lightening flashed, and a moment later the thunder would be heard pealing across the water like a signal of distress. The vapor seemed to gather from all sides and a few minutes after sunset the sky was covered. Not a single star on which to hang our hopes; the wind was rising and the huge billows gave out a phosphorescent glare that showed their outlines dimly as they rose in our wake momentarilly threatening the destruction of our tiny craft. What appeared to be balls of pale green fire were frequently noticed in the water. These were probably the dimly seen forms of some of the numerous species of luminous fish, that inhabit these regions, but whatever the cause, the mysterious light added not a little to the wildness of the scene. Now and then a roller of ambitious proportions would climb over the stern and distribute itself about the deck. Uunder such circumstances the ocean seems very large, the boat very small—a two inch plank between you and eternity—these were many dangerous reefs along the coast and some isolated rocks, but in the awful blackness of the night nothing was visible, except when illuminated for an instant by the lightning, which was frequent, and it was to this finally that we owed our preservation. About midnight we were alarmed by a sound like muffled thunder, but continuous, a dull roar that was easily heard above the tumult of the storm.

The captain understood at once that we were driving straight into the breakers. The force of the wind and the swell of the sea had carried us several points to the leeward. The old sailor knew every inch of the coast, and under ordinary circumstances would have passed these dangerous points in safety, no matter how dark the night, but he had not been able to cope with the elements. We had been driven far out of our course. As it was, our only hope lay in steering through a narrow passage between two masses of rock that rose out of the sea like a ruined castle. This narrow opening was scarcely wide enough to admit a small boat and, of course, was quite invisible in the darkness, but we must risk it. The sound of the breakers became more and more distinct. Our chances were very slight indeed. Should our frail vessel strike these rocks she would be reduced to splinters in a few minutes, that the danger was imminent could not be denied, our captain held his place at the helm—motionless—speechless—rigid as an image of stone. The thunder of the breakers grew more teriffic every moment, while we were all but smothered by the deluge of salt spray—we clung to the rigging with the grip of despair—out of the blackness Death whispered hoarsely, "welcome, welcome!" It was during this awful hour, when one's mind ought to have been concentrated on spiritual matters, that the writer found himself the victim of a common delusion known as "living over the past"—and I confess with shame that the review revealed little to be proud of—strangely enough, the pictures recalled belonged to the period of childhood or early youth—again I smoked my first "cheroot" back of a deserted house, hidden among a wilderness of weeds—once more, I "reaped" where I had not "sown," at least that was the testimony of an irate farmer who presented a bill to my astonished

ROCKS OF COAST OF RUHTAIV.

parent for fruits that had never been ordered—in fact it seemed that the life of the victim, had been made up of a series of wicked and unlawful acts, one of the most disreputable of which seemed to stand out with a distinctness that eclipsed all others.

Trembling on the verge of a waterary grave, all present surroundings were forgotten, the author was a boy once more, it was a lovely morning in March; a sharp frost the previous night had bridged the streams with a thin film of ice which rang like steel as we skipped stones across the shinny surface, however, this melted rapidly under the warm rays of the sun–it was the sugar making season in northern Ohio. Four school boys had found excuses sufficiently plausible to secure their freedom, they were now approaching a "camp" near the village—they did not seem to understand that the manufacture of maple molasses was carried on for profit, and when they found the place deserted, it occured to them that it would be a pleasant experiment to "boil down" a few gallons of sap until it acquired that peculiar quality known as "wax"—with this laudable object in view, one of the number began to gather wood, another carried the water, the third washed the pan and made ready for the work, while the fourth sinner whose name shall never be known, was appointed to the important service of scout, with instructions to give the alarm in case of danger.

Number one was John H———d, number two, Jerome B———n, number three, George McC———h, number four—unknown.

The property lay immediately west of the village cemetery and had been leased for the season by a pious old man locally known as "Dad Burnit"—"Dad" was a member of the church, a consistent, hard working christian, whose conscientious scruples forbade the use of profanity under the most trying circumstances, but who, nevertheless, found it absolutely necessary at times, to give vent to his feelings or die from suffocation, he therefore invented the mild expression quoted above, by which, from long association became recognized for miles around.

The unnamed member of this quartet of depradators stationed himself on a fence and watched five minutes—from a nearby hedge came the song of a sparrow—the creek hills were velled by a bluish mist that softened their rugged outlines—a chipmonk scampered across an open space: number four gave one sharp, scrutinizing glance around the horizon—all was as peaceful as a dream—surely there could be no danger: he could hear the voices of number one, two and three talking in low tones: he could also see the smoke, now slowly rising out of the underbrush: surely it could do no harm to look after that chipmonk—the chase proved long and exciting, even the "wax" was forgotten—and number four seemed quite oblivious of the fact that he was in any way connected with the enterprise, however, his responsibility as sentry was suddenly recalled———there was a tremendous shout. "Dad Burnit, don't run—er I'll fill yer so full of holes you won't make a decent shadder." Number four was paralyzed with fright and stood like a statue, unable to move, number one, two and three were affected differently, they fled like the wind, making for the cemetery where they escaped, hiding among the tombs—while the unfortunate sentry was dragged back to town, down through the main street to his fathers door, and the story of his infamy told with many outbursts of indignation on the part of the narrator—of course he received such punishment as was deemd proper under the circumstances, but the unkindest cut of all, came in the evening when his three accomplices returned with a pan full of "wax" which they had made in undisturbed security while their companion was being ignominously marched off to the village; the sorrow of remorse of that moment all came back on this memorable night, and the roar of wind and waves was drowned by the dreadful shout of old "Dad Burnit," and the regret of a misspent life was lost in the deeper regret of that day in March, thirty years ago, not regret for the sin, but for the loss of his share in the spoils—this confession is made in the interest of science—not because the writer cares to expose his unregenerate heart to the gaze of the world—can any one explain the phenomena? He truly wished to think of things that were good, but at that supreme moment he could think of nothing but the "wax"—that he failed to secure. Suddenly a vivid flash, followed by another, revealed our position. The illumination lasted only a fraction of a second but it was enough for the captain to determine the location of the narrow strait, into which we were soon driving, the keel grazing the wall in its passage, which would certainly have proved our destruction had it not been for the timely flash. Once through this channel the sea became smoother and we felt comparatively safe. Everything loose had been washed overboard. Kettle, bucket, water cask; even our tin plates and drinking cups had dissapeared. These things had been overlooked in the hurry to secure the hatches the evening before. It was well that this was our last night on the sloop, as our meals would have been pitifully slim after this loss. Roland mounred the fate of his huge dinner pot and refused to be comforted. He felt that no other could ever take its place, and he dwelt long and lovingly on its peculiar qualities recalling the miraculous stews that had been concocted in its dark depths.

About four o'clock we entered the harbor of Puerto Cortez, the second time, in a gale that sent the waters swhirling almost to the doors of the custom house. About six o'clock a couple of officers rowed out where we lay rocking on the short choppy sea, and, having examined our documents we were permitted to land. We were thoroughly drenched, having slept none during the night, consequently were not in a particularly good humor. It seemed an age since we left Utillia, and it was nearly a month before we entirely recovered from the peculiar sensation caused by the constant motion of the sloop—for days the earth seemed to be slowly heaving like the sea; when we closed our eyes we imagined we could feel the floor of the hotel rising and falling like the deck of the vessel. After a good bath, a complete change of clothing and a cup of black coffee brewed by our old friend, the hostess of the "Hotel American," we felt much refreshed and set at once about our preparations for the overland journey. The captain and Roland only lingered long enough to replace the lost utensils and hurriedly bade us adieu. They were anxious to return to their families; who would naturally be alarmed, on account of the storm which broke so soon after we left the harbor.

We felt like very old friends indeed, although our acquaintance extended over a period of less than sixty days, it seemed to us that we had known these honest sailors all our lives, and it was with genuine regret we bade them adieu.

It is wonderful how quickly men of widely different circumstances become attached to each other when exposed to common dangers; for weeks we had shared alike the pleasures and perils of the little sloop, together we had partaken of the strange dishes invented by Roland, "the genius of the skillet," as the captain dubbed him, together we had sizzled under the burning sky during those calms that have already been referred to, together we had plowed the midnight sea when every moment seemed an hour and every hour an age—but it was over at last and the experience forms a figure in the ever lengthening pattern that falls from memories looms; looms whose busy shuttles never cease gathering up the parti-colored threads of our lives; light and dark, bright or somber. We part at the wharf. We will not say good bye—only 'so long, we'll see you later." Of course we never expected to but somehow its easier to part that way.

As rapidly as possible we made our preparations for the mountain trip. When at last everything was packed and delivered to the railroad company, we sat down to wait for a train. While waiting, we explored the neighborhood in search of "pines" and found some—this recalls a little lecture recently delivered by a "Hoosier School Master" for the benefit of the children under his charge in which he gravely informed his interested listeners that pineapples grew on pine trees, calling attention to the close resemblance of the "apple" to the cones with which the boys and girls were familiar, the difference in size and quality being due, he declared to climatic influence; he did not say that the natives trained monkeys to climb these trees and bring down the fruit, though that would not have been more absurd—we do not like to dispute so high an authority but a strict adherence to the facts compels us to state that pineapples do not grow on pine trees —or trees of any description but on a lowly plant which attains a height of from 3 to 4 feet. The cultivation of this fruit is one of the profitable industries of the south—the crop is very sure, and pays quite as well as bananas—the following extract from the "Honduras Almanac" is the result of many years successful experience by an English planter.

A PINE TREE, HEIGHT 4 FEET.

"The climate must be moist with a damp soil; as it does not "seed," this plant "is propagated by suckers, requiring only from 12 to 18 months to realize on the first crop—they should be planted in rich red soil, about 18 inches apart and carefully weeded about every three months—careful cultivation greatly improves the flavor of the fruit.

"The distance apart at which they are planted in Jamiaca is 3 1-2 feet between rows and 2½ feet in the rows, this gives 4,840 plants to the acre, out of this number you can safely count on 4,000 perfect pines, these sold at the very low price of 5 cents would give the producer an income of $200.00 per acre every 16 or 18 months. The pine fields ought to be cleaned five or six times a year, each cleaning costing say, $5 per acre, or from $25 to $30 per acre per annum, this constitutes the whole cultivation. Each plant produces one "pine," its place is then taken by one of the numerous suckers, the superfluous ones being carefully removed; only those who have tested the pine apple when fully matured in its native home have any idea of its delicious qualities, it is without doubt the finest of all southern fruits. We might add for the information of those who are interested in the subject that the varieties best adapted for export are the black Antigua, black Jamaica or "cow-boy," the Ripley, Charlotte Rothschild, smooth Cayenne, scarlet (or Cuban) and British Queen. Northern visitors are astonished at the size this fruit attains under proper cultivation, many specimens weighing from 10 to 12 pounds.

GUARDIAN OF THE PEACE, BELIZE.

CHAPTER VI.

THE GREAT TRANS-CONTINENTAL RAILROAD—A FLYING TRIP OVER THE SAME—TOWN OF SAN PEDRO—A SMALL EARTHQUAKE, MERELY A SAMPLE—WAITING.

The reader who will take the trouble to consult the map of Central America, published by Rand, McNally & Co., will notice a long black line drawn across the republic of Honduras. It begins at Puerto Cortez and ends at a point on the Pacific near Amapala, or vice versa, as the observer may decide. It represents the railroad which was to become "America's highway" and which, to use the flowery language of its enthusiastic promoters, was to "shape the destiny of the nation."

The rich agricultural regions of the interior would be opened to the world, and the tide of prosperity that would follow could hardly be imagined much less described. An elaborate system of feeders were planned that would tap all those rich mining centers, which lacked only transportation facilities to transform them into veritable bonanzas. Hundreds of thousands of acres of land, almost worthless from a commercial point of view, would find a market at prices that made the unsuspecting native fairly dizzy with anticipation. For a while the little republic endulged in rosy visions of wealth, the humblest citizens would become millionaires, bamboo huts and 'dobe walls would be replaced by palaces of marble. Alas for Central American enterprise! The natives gazed a moment on these busy preparations with a sort of wild surprise, then with a murmured "Manana" sank back in their hammocks to slumber and dream.

Not so the scheming contractors, who "worked" the government for all it was worth—and more. A small army of men were employed and operations began on the northern division, while the attention of the country was centered on this scene of activity, the wiley agents of a syndicate of English Bankers were no less busy at the capitol negotiating a loan, by which the state became responsible to the amount of $27,000,000. This deal having been successfully accomplished, it suddenly dawned on the projectors that the plan of building a road across the mountains was not feasible at that time. The workmen were laid off, "temporarily" with instructions to be in readiness to report at a moments notice. A quarter of a century has passed and they are still waiting with that patience that is characteristic of the Spanish American. Meanwhile the ardent advocates of the enterprise dissappeared, leaving thirty-six or thirty-seven miles of poorly constructed narrow gauge track as a slight compensation for the millions they carried away. Over this wretched remnant of a great "transcontinental railroad" toy cars are dragged by a toy locomotive, covering the distance from the port to San Pedro in from three to ten hours, according to the condition of the lame engine, and its native fireman. Trains do not arrive or depart at regular intervals, but are dispatched

CHURCH SAN PEDRO.

whenever a sufficient amount of freight has accumulated to warrant such extravagance. So the restless traveler may have to wait one, two, or three days for a chance to risk his life on this, the worse bit of railroad in existence. The risk is not from reckless speed or danger of collisions or that the train may jump the track, or from any of the usual accidents of railway travel—it is that you may die from starvation before reaching your destination, or be devoured by mosquitoes during one of those half day stops in the midst of a swamp where the air is darkened by swarms of these persistent insects, or that you may be tempted to destroy one or two of the officials, or in the enthusiasm of the moment you might even sacrifice the conductor or a brakeman, and thus bring down the vengence of the law, which is administered in such a loose and partial manner that you would most likely be swiftly convicted and sentenced to serve thirty days as a first class passenger!

We had all our traps carried over to the depot and paid for transportation at the rate of 1 1-2 cents per pound for the thirty-six miles, a rate just three times that charged by the Steamship Co., from New York, a distance of three thousand miles. The tariff seemed a trifle high at first, but when we struck the overland express and planked down twelve cents a pound on goods billed for Tegucigalpa, a distance of only 180 miles, or seven days journey by mule, you will readily understand why so common an article as beer commands 50 cents for a very small glass in the capitol city. However, it's not considered a wholesome beverage and some poor people are forced to drink water.

In about two days a sufficient amount of freight had been gathered in to justify the making up of a train, and presently a little locomotive, guiltless of stack or "cow catcher," was brought forth and after much coughing, wheezing and sputtering, it was finally coaxed into making a start. Our train consisted of one coach, and a flat car, the latter for the accomodation of the bales of goods destined for the interior, which were covered with a huge tarpaulin, the former, an abandoned box car, had been converted to its present use by placing a plank seat on either side, lengthwise of the coach, to strengthen the illusion a row of square openings had been cut in the sides, through which the mosquitos came in to cheer the weary passengers with their tuneful melodies —this elegant equipage was filled to the point of suffocation. The passengers were mostly natives, who were not lavishly dressed— men, women and children, they carried all manner of bundles, every foot of space was occupied. We were packed like herrings in a box. Every one smoked, which added to the comfort of the trip. We made fine time at the start whizzing along at the rate of 12 miles an hour, but had to make a long stop at the "lagoon" for repairs and to take on sand to be used on the "grade." While waiting, we walked ahead a mile or two studying the scenery. At last the train overtook us. We scrambled to our places and sped on our way, plunging into the forest of cahune palms. Here the tall trees met overhead, almost shutting out the light and the effect was like entering a tunnel. The smoke was stifling. On each side of the track were shallow pools of

 water, stretching away into the gloomy shades of the wilderness, dead and glassy. Suddenly the train came to a stand. Every one was out in a moment. What was the cause of delay? It was hardly worth mentioning, the track had sunk in the mire and we must wait until it could be straightened up and new ties procured. It was now that some of the party indulged in language that would scorch this page if transcribed. It is therefore omitted.

Only those who have tarried in the midst of tropical swamps, can form an idea of the torture inflicted during those two hours by the swarms of stinging insects that literally filled the air. The natives squated on the tracks, smoking stolidly, their dull expressionless faces betrayed not the slightest emotion. When the mosquitoes would accumulate to the depth of half an inch, they would slowly rub them off and silently wait for the next crop.

Choloma is a way station consisting of a cluster of huts in the woods, but it boasts of a telegraph office, "telegrafo nacional"—as we expected to reach the capitol in the course of a few weeks we thought it proper to warn the citizens of the impending invasion, and at the same time experiment with tropical electricity, having been informed it was subject to the drowsy influence of the climate —we therefore prepared the following modest message, "Hotel American, Tegucipalpa, a party of hungry gringoes will reach your place in six weeks, please order dinner at once"—this was translated and delivered to the operator who proceeded to play on the instrument with the ease of professional—click—click—clickat—tick—tack—clickety clack—clack—his action was admirable, his time perfect, the music ran smoothly along without a jar or break —certainly we had made sure of one square meal, with ample time for its preparation—months later, while stopping at the hotel in question the landlord handed us a "telegrafo" which he had just received, it was our request for an early dinner, it had been re-translated from the barbarous Spanish: "Some tengo hambre gringos will be come, want comida muches quick, como no! beware, ahora luege," it was presented to the writer and is treasured as a curious example of electrical degeneration. Miss Anna

J. Somers, a bright young lady of Indianapolis, recently returned from an excursion to San Pedro Sula, recalls an incident that occured at this station; while waiting for the inevitable repairs, she was unfortunate enough to catch a bit of cinder in her eye—she suffered intensely—all efforts to remove the particle only increased the pain—she was becoming greatly alarmed when a handsome young Spaniard approached, who with many apologies for the intrusion begged to be allowed to lend his assistance—under such circumstances she was only to glad to receive aid from any source—leading her to a seat he requested that she lean back closing the well eye, very carefully he raised the lid of the other, in a moment he located the piece of grit, then suddenly stooping 'till his face touched her own, he thrust his tongue in her eye—the

MASON'S CONCEPTION OF A EARTHQUAKE.

operation was over in an instant, the offensive substance was removed, and all pain ceased at once. While trying to think of the appropriate Spanish words to properly express her thanks, her friend withdrew, smiling and bowing until lost to view—when too late the word "gracias" came to her which she has since elaborated to "muches gracias, senor," by an odd co-incidence, one of Miss Somers young lady companions met with a similar mishap at this same station on their return trip—but the good looking specialist was not to be found—was it altogether an accident?

At last the road was repaired, the train started slowly, cautiously, and for the rest of the way we averaged about four miles an hour. When we got through the swamp we struck the "grade."

Some trees had fallen across the track. A stop of an hour was required to remove these obstacles. Then began the ascent—puff —puff—puff. Two Indians were detailed to go ahead and sprinkle the rails with sand, but it seemed almost impossible for the crippled engine to do its work. The passengers dismounted and one good-natured fellow offered to help "push the thing along," but his services were politely declined, so we walked ahead stopping now and then to test the bananas that hung in tempting proximity to the road. At each of these plantations stacks of fruit were corded up much, as we see wood along some of our roads in the States. On its return the train would stop at these places and carry the produce to the port, where it would be re-stacked under long, low sheds, to await the steamer from New Orleans.

In the course of an hour or two the "grade" was overcome and we took our places once more in the coach. The engineer pulled the throttle to its widest extent, the fireman piled coal and wood  into the furnace until it glowed with a white heat. The ground was now solid, the track in fair condition and the last few minutes we attained a speed of 15 miles an hour, rushing into San Pedro with a wild scream that brought all the idlers of the village to the depot. Here we were met by a host of men and boys who insisted on carrying everything we had, regardless of our remonstrations, but we finally fought them off and made a bargain with a poor old fellow who possessed an ancient Mexican cart, to which was attached a team of the saddest looking oxen we ever beheld. For the consideration of two reals, he conveyed our luggage to the "Posado De Renaud," a small but comfortable hostelry.

San Pedro is the only town between the coast and Tegucigalpa possessing a hotel, excepting the "American" at Comyagua.

Beside the Renaud House, there is the "Hotel Americano," under the management of Mr. Louie Seifert, a German of progressive ideas. Here you could enjoy the luxury of a cool bath, to say nothing of iced water and other mild drinks. San Pedro shows many signs of improvement. The old houses are being replaced by modern frame structures. A firm of American carpenters, Messrs. Coleman & Barnes, having revolutionized the building business. The railroad, wretched as it is, serves to keep open communication with the world, and brings the newspapers every week, the result is an air of bustle and commotion quite out of keeping with the traditions of the country.* A rude system of water works supplies the town from a spring in the mountains. At an elevation of several hundred feet, a reservoir has been built from which pipes are laid on the surface of the ground and thus carried to various convenient points, where public hydrants are placed, here you will always find a crowd of women with there water jars, patiently waiting their turn, the while smoking and chatting, possibly discussing matters of dress, or lack of it.

As in most other Central American towns, we find the male children, under 10 or 12 years of age, quite unincumbered, so far as clothing is concerned and their appearance on the corners, or in the plaza, where groups are engaged in games of marble, or ball, attract the attention of the stranger.

San Pedro is delightfully situated on a plain at the foot of a range of mountains, whose blue outlines are visible far out at sea and whose cloud-like forms we had often discussed from the deck of the Seagull. From that distance they looked very beautiful, the pale blue of the sunlit sides melting imperceptably into the violet shadows; sometimes at sunset their crests seemed tipped with gold, the effect being produced by the reflection of the yellow light from the rocky precipices. Again in the early morning they would loom up through the purple mist like shadows on the eastern sky, changing every moment with the increasing light, but always like a vision, a dream, no suggestion of rocks and precipices and miles of wilderness, with foaming torrents that must be crossed as best we may—but now we are here, their hard reality becomes apparent. We can see the dark forests, the walls of rock, the path winding up the steep side like a yellow thread until quite lost among the pines. Almost daily their crests were obscured by masses of black clouds. From the midst of the dark shaddows

---

*Since the above was written this famous road has been taken in hand by a company of Americans, who have practically rebuilt the portion connecting Puerto Cortez and San Pedro, and continued the line as far as Pimiento, about sixty-one miles from the coast. Trains run up one day and down the next, making fairly good time. My informant also states that the pier has been reconstructed, and vessels now come alongside and transfer their load to the cars direct.

ruddy lightnings played and the rumble of the thunder could be plainly heard echoing from peak to peak.

It was at this place that we first noticed the shelves in stores guarded by wires stretched along in front of them, at least all those containing goods of a breakable nature. We wondered at this at first, but soon learned the cause. We were now in a country subject to frequent earthquake shocks, which would tumble glass or queensware to the floor, causing great loss and annoyance. Occasionally the shocks are so severe that buildings suffer and life itself is endangered by the sudden collapsing of the massive 'dobe walls, or falling of the heavy tile roofs. We used to think we would enjoy an earthquake and had looked forward to the time when we might experience one, but somehow when we arrived on the ground we lost all desire to investigate the phenomona. We were quite satisfied with what we had read, and with the explanations of those who had made the subject a special study. But we were to have a real shake, and will say right here that the single experience quite convinced us that there is nothing to be gained by an intimate acquaintance with an earthquake; in fact, we know much less than we did before. We used to have well defined theories on the subject, we have none now—at least none worth advertising.

POSADO DE REYNAUD.

There was no preliminary rumbling, or slight tremor—the shock came with the suddenness of an explosion—the crash of falling crockery and tumbling furniture was appalling, to this was added the screams of women and children, as they rushed madly for doors or windows in a frantic effort to escape from under those awful roofs. The confusion and terror of that hour cannot be described—clocks struck out of time, bells clanged discordantly, nameless horror and hopeless despair was painted on every face— we were no exception to the rule—and whatever ideas we possessed concerning cause and effect as applied to seismic disturbances left us to return to return no more—it was over in less than three minutes—those brief moments comprised an age—the whole population fled to the plaza, where they fell, some on their faces, some on their knees and prayed—loudly, incoherently—some for forgiveness—others for immediate deliverance—the latter class seem to predominate—very few seem troubled about their sins—their only thought was present safety—the sensation was peculiar it seemed as though the earth's crust was only about an inch thick and liable to break through at any moment—it quiverd under us like thin ice—how longingly we gazed up into the clear blue sky and wished for wings, instead of feet—but there was no retreating—so we simply stood there as lightly as possible, and felt sorry—there were some strange grinding sounds now, that may have come from the sky above, or the depths below, we did not attempt to locate them. We were scared—too badly scared to note accurately time or circumstance. One thought came to us as we listened trembling to the chorus of payers, that where being hurled heavenward, so as to speak, by that crowd of frightened beings, whose every day language was marked by a rich profusion of words of topical import. That single thought was this: What an addition a small earthquake would be to an ordinary religious revival, what a wholesale conversion of souls would take place—souls long since dead to all the commonplace methods of ministers. When the solid earth begins to roll like the sea, and tall trees bow their heads to the dust, and mysterious sounds fill the air, when birds flutter helplessly to the ground, and cattle stand with legs far apart, eyes dilated with terror—then it is that ones early religious training asserts itself, strong men are seen to weep like children and cry aloud to heaven for protection—yes an earthquake is a wonderful stimulus to religious fervor.

The next day the occurance was forgotten. No great damage had been done. Some old cracked walls showed wider seams, some dishes were broken, some clocks toppled off shelves and damaged. What seemed so terrible was but a slight disturbance, and the day following business resumed its normal conditions, the saloons were running as usual; the men who prayed so lustily a few hours since might now be found in their accustomed haunts playing poker and decorating the surrounding territory with a dark brown fresco of tobacco juice and abandoned quids, while their conversation was adorned with the usual amount of invective —invective peculiar to the climate, rankly luxuriant like the vegetation—dark, dank, dense.

We stopped at this place several weeks, in fact we were forced to do so, as it was necessary to secure mules and mozos; the latter must be well posted on the roads and mountain passes. The first must be sound and true. we were delayed at every step by the eternal "Manana." Tomorrow! Tomorrow! The native Hondurian has ten thousand excuses for delay. He only asks one day but usually succeeds in taken seven. They cannot understand why anyone should be in haste. To hurry with these people is to be vulgar. In this respect the Hondurian is wonderfully like the Japanese, whose "Tadaima," translated "By and By" or "after a while," simply means an indefinite postponemont of whatever you have on hand. "A little later." "another day,"

While the universal "Manana" of the Spaniard is represented exactly by the Japanese word ',Miyouichi" (tomorrow,) and is used with the same exasperating coolness. "Don't be in a hurry" says the Jap, "there will be another day." Never do anything to-day that can be put off till tomorrow," says the native of Hondurus," because something might happen that would make it unnecessary and the labor would be lost," which would be sad indeed. The people can bear the loss of time, money, wife or child, with a heroic fortitude that is touching, but the thought of labor wasted breaks their hearts.

While waiting we strolled about the place taking notes. By referring to my memorandum, I find under August first the following observation : "From the office window I can see a native woman at a wash tub. She is bare-headed and her unconfined raven locks fall below her waist, but she is not handsome. Her skin is the color of copper, her face has less expression than a board fence—and, to sum it up, she has no sense. If she had why would she stand there rubbing away for hours under the blistering August sun, when by moving her bench four feet—actually not an inch more–she would come within the broad shadow of a mango tree through whose dense foliage scarcely a ray of light can pass. Even her parrot shows his intelligence by perching among its cooling shadows, while a cat lies asleep at its foot.

It is so with everything else. It is simply lack of intelligence among the masses of the inhabitants that makes the first discovered country of America the last to be settled and civilized. No other country in the world can boast of greater natural resources or climatic advantages, not only surpassingly beautiful to the eye, but possessing a deep, rich soil, capable of producing (according to altitude) every fruit known to the tropic or temperate zones, to say nothing of vegetables and cereals, while its mineral wealth is beyond computation. Those who have given the subject careful consideration declare that the state of Honduras is without doubt one of the richest countries in the world; but leaving these two great sources of wealth entirely out of our calculation, her native woods alone will more than pay the national debt. The whole story is told in three words, lack of sense. Right across the street a man is sawing wood. He has a good saw, such as every American farmer owns. Can you immagine how he uses this convenient tool? He holds it between his knees and rubs the sticks up and down over the sharp teeth until he can break them. This is a fair illustration of the way they do things down here.

August 2.—Signs of improvement have been noted. Honduras is not without hope. At Truxillo three boys were discovered fighting over a game of marbles. At Puerto Cortez, a youngster was seen throwing at a dog, and at San Pedro a progressive youth was found spinning a top in an alley. Only those who have seen the death like stupor that prevails among the smaller children, can appreciate these slight evidences of the awakening of natural instincts among members of the rising generation.

That these three examples of youthful enterprise occured at points widely separated, is a hopeful indication. This shows that the influence is not confined to one locality but is in the air. When you see the *children* of a nation waking up—look out!"

PREPARING TO MOUNT

CHAPTER VII.

SERVICES OF MOSES AND AARON SECURED—FINAL ARRANGEMENTS FOR THE OVERLAND TRIP—THE START—AMONG THE MOUNTAINS—DISERTATION ON HAMMOCKS— SANTA CRUZE AND ITS MINES—BEAUTIFUL SCENERY—PRIMITIVE VILLAGES.

San Pedro contains no buildings of importance, an old church, of plainest pattern — its plastered walls cracked and broken, bearing on their rough surface the record of earthquakes and revolutions for two generations or more—a new cabildo entirely too modern to be graceful or picturesque, and altogether out of harmony with its surroundings.

But the town is not without pleasant features, one of these, is found in the streams of clear water that cross the

HIGH BRIDGE.

village from east to west, at intervals of two or three hundred yards, one of them ran through the lot within a few feet of the dining room, and its cheerful music added not a little to the pleasure of the guest stopping at the Posado de Renaud.

The servant question now demanded immediate settlement—we must have guides or mozos, and they must be expert packers, and besides know every path leading through that stretch of mountain wilderness that extends for leauges to the southward.

We therefore began the search, and for some time met with little encouragement, very few cared to take so long a trip—they objected to going more than a dozen leagues, and few had ever been farther away from their homes—wages was no object, as they could live without work—so why engage in toilsome marches, for the paltry consideration of a few silver dollars? Besides it meant separation from their families for an indefinite period—we found these people strongly attached to their homes, and disinclined to engage in any enterprise that would carry them beyond the small circle of their daily experience—which meant a little work with much leisure for music, cigarettes, and hours in the restful hammock—happy natives, would that the world might know something of the contentment that fills their peaceful days—every one had some valid excuse to offer and we were almost discouraged, when we ran across a couple of wild fellows from the department of Olancho, of which it has been said, "Olancho, ancho para intrar, angosta para salir" (easy to enter, hard to leave.) In fact this department is noted for its desperadoes and general lawlessness —these hardy mountaineers, young and strong, were ready for any kind of adventure, and expressed a desire to see the pacific coast— they were a murderous looking pair, but we promptly engaged them—they were tall and handsome, but their black eyes flashed with a peculiar fire—they were very dark, with shocks of hair trimmed after a fashion peculiar to the country, short behind, long in front, this sable foretop hanging low over their foreheads, gave them a particularly sinister expression—each man was armed with a revolver and a long machete, recently ground and polished, these convenient tools were supported by a stout belt of leather; they wore broad sombreros, red shirts, blue trousers, rolled to their knees—they were evidently looked upon as "bad men" by the villagers, who regarded all Olanchans with suspicion if not with fear—but what we admired most about these ruffians was their readiness—they invented no excuses for delay—and never so much as murmered "Mauana," but were ready to start at any moment, and to prove their willingness, they set out at once to hunt up animals and we were astonished at their success. The very next day they appeared before the posado with a train of fourteen mules, which they had taken possession of, telling the owners to come around at a certain hour and get their money. They were the most successful stock buyers we had ever met and we were delighted with their direct business methods. We noticed that they handled their weapons very carelessly and whenever the owner of a mule was disposed to ask an exorbitant price, their fingers played nervously over the triggers of those huge revolvers in a way that somehow seemed to end the controversy, and the dealer appeared glad to close the contract and cheerfully signed a receipt in full. The price of sound riding mules at that time was $100 and good packs $75 to $80. One was secured at $60, the reduction being made on account of age. The more we saw of these fellows the better we liked them. They carried long unpronounceable Indian names, which we could never learn so we called them simply Moses and Aaron, not that they in in the least resembled those famous characters, but because the names were easy to call and remember. They seemed pleased with the titles which they evidently considered as a special mark of respect or honor, the equivalent of General, Colonel, Doctor or Professor. Besides being an expert packer, Aaron had other accomplishments that he was very proud of, he could write and sketch, and besides understood English—or thought he did—true his language was rather disjointed at times, and his chirography somewhat faulty according to the spencerian standard, nevertheless his skill in this direction was quite remarkable, when his opportunities were considered—if his vocabulary was not extensive, he used his stock to the best advantage, as the reader will see by the examples presented herewith.

We consider sketch number one much the best, the lines are drawn with confidence, there is no hesitation, no faltering, and if the artist betrays his ignorance of anatomy, he is not troubled on that account; he has certainly succeeded in catching the spirit of Pizarro, and after all that's the main thing—we don't know who the excited individual in the distance is intended to represent, but if it's meant for pizarro's owner it's a mean slander that's all—by "front pros-

NO. 1—MULE.

pect" Aaron means simply a front view.

Sketch number two is not as strong as number one, he has given to much attention to detail, the building in the distance is a school house and the teacher has dismissed the pupils in order that they may watch the "Gringo" learn to ride—the party at the extreme right is supposed to be the author of these remincinces—the position is neither graceful nor dignified and is hereby branded a base libel—Aaron will do more sketching for us!

Bills of sale having been duly made out and receipted, the boys at once began the packing process. Some of the animals were young and frisky and did not take kindly to the operation. One particularly vicious colt rolled and kicked until he scattered his load in every direction. This exhibition attracted a large crowd of idlers who observed the proceedings with interest. The performance was not particularly reassuring to the writer, who looked forward to the hour of mounting one of those wild beasts, with a good deal of trepidation, and he remembers with what solicitude he approached the particular animal set apart for his use.

At last the packing was completed and Moses and Aaron, with a faithful servant, Santiago, set off with the train, one day in advance of the principals. This arrangement was made partly to allow us time to settle up our business in the town and partly that we might enjoy our first mountain ride undisturbed by the clatter of the muleteers, besides our animals, with no burdens but their riders, would make much better time than the "cargoes," therefore we would easily overtake the train sometime next day.

It was here that we had our hammocks made, and laid in all those articles essential to comfort on a long journey through an almost un-inhabited wilderness. Huge Mexican saddles were procured with holsters attached for the pistols, that every one is expected to carry; leggins and savage spurs of shining brass, huge leghorn sombreros decorated with wide ribbons, these were secured by a stout cord tied to our belts to prevent them from going over the mountains when struck by the playful breezes that lurk among those lofty passes among the clouds.

Everything must come to an end, and so our stay in this pleasant village. The time had arrived when I must mount that mule. Only those who have never been on a horse's back can realize with what caution I now approached the sleepy looking creature tied up in the rear of the hotel. I felt strangely cramped and awkward, with the tight fitting leggings and jingling spurs, and the knowledge that my good friend, Mrs. Renaud, had marshalled the entire female force in the kitchen to witness our departure, did not add to my ease; besides these young ladies, whom I knew were enchanging many nods and winks behind the lattice, a half dozen old travelers were ranged around the yard to say good bye, or wish us "God speed." I would willingly have dispensed with these pleasant ceremonies and will here acknowledge that I offered a boy $2.00 to lead the mule a mile out of the town and tie it to a tree where it might easily be found, but he refused. So, as there was no other way, I approached the beast with as great a show of assurance as I could assume, and throwing the rein over my arm placed my hand on the pummel of the saddle, my left foot in the stirrup and made a wild leap, landing squarely on the animal's back the first time. The mule exhibited some signs of surprise and walked around the inclosure once or twice on his hind feet, pawing the air, then he suddenly reversed his tactics and made the circle a couple times on his fore feet, his heels playing with the clouds. I felt that my title to the exalted position I now enjoyed was very slim indeed. However, the wild screams of men and maids added not little to my determination to "stay with him," and after a ten minute struggle the old fellow seemed perfectly satisfied that his rider had legal rights that could not be disputed, and we started on our journey, our ears filled with the applause of the multitude.

From his bold and chivalrous spirit, his untiring energy and love of enterprise, I named my newly acquired property, Pizarro. As a conqueror he ranks well with his illustrious predecessor.

It is wonderful how soon one becomes attached to the dumb servant who toils along so patiently, carrying the rider in safety over paths that one would hardly attempt on foot.

In this country the traveler steps out of the village into the wilderness. One is struck by the absence of cultivated fields —only the "forest pruneval", the huge trees were overhung with vines or overgrown with air plants of which many varieties abound. Some orchids of rare beauty were noted in this neighborhood.

The path, for the most part only wide enough for a single

rider, followed a zigzag course, each "tack" carrying us a little nearer to the summit of the mountain. The tall trees met over our heads and the silence and gloom of this wilderness was impressive. There was no hum of insects, no bird music—only the melancholy sighing of the wind as it swayed the tops of the trees. Great banners of Spanish moss of a silvery gray color depended from the branches. Now and then a flock of green parrots would cross our path, and once we saw a pair of maccaws. These most brilliant of tropical birds, like their green coated cousins, are quite devoid of melody, though their voices are coarser and their whole life seems to be passed in an endless quarrel.

We arrived at the "cumbre" or summit about noon, where we stopped for lunch and to look back over the country which lay

NO. 2—MULE.

below us like a map. The village of San Pedro was plainly visible. Its red tiled roofs and white washed walls gleaming prettily out of the sea of green that surrounded it like an ocean. With this single exception, the forest was unbroken. Far away to the right a faint streak of silvery brightness betrayed the presence of the Ulua, but most distant of all, and rising against the horizon like a dark blue wall, was the Gulf of Mexico, fully forty miles away. After an hours rest we continued our journey. We were now descending into the valley of the chamelecon and found the road rougher and more difficult. My affection for Pizarro increased perceptably. We rounded some curves where a false step would have sent us tumbling hundreds of feet over rocky precipices. Again we descended declivities that would have discouraged a squirrel, but our good mules carefully measured each step, avoiding stone or stick, never placing a foot until perfectly satisfied that it would not slip. At one place we crossed a deep ravine on a log about 18 inches wide, the top of which had been flattened by hewing away the rough bark. Far below a mountain torrent roared among the rocks. The scene was wild and beautiful but I must acknowledge that *one* rider took little interest in its charms while swinging on that frail bridge. Shortly after this we found ourselves in a valley with broad openings, the grass responding to the recent rains, was just assuming a delicate shade of green, giving the country a parklike appearance. Clumps of oak, with wide spreading branches were scattered over the plain, a clear stream flowed peacefully between verdant banks. Here and there we noted isolated piles of rocks overgrown with vines many of them of rich flowering varieties. Between the trees, lovely vistas stretched away to where the mountains rose dimly, a wall of blue flecked by the slowly moving shadows of clouds that begin to gather shortly after noon, but in all its wide extent, not a cottage was seen, not a garden plot, not a sign of human activity. In places the gnarled and twisted oaks took the form of old apple trees and so perfect was the illusion that we could not help looking for the farm house which we felt sure must be somewhere near. Here we heard the familiar whistle of the "Bobwhite," clear and shrill as in the orchards of Indiana. Night fell suddenly while we were yet wandering in this plain, where scarcely a trace of any path could be found. Being entirely unacquainted with the road, we dropped the reins and trusted ourselves to the guidance of our enterprising beasts, whose early morning exhibition had attracted so much attention. Forty miles over rough mountain passes seemed to have a quieting effect, and the general now plodded along sedately enough. To make it worse, heavy clouds overspread the sky, the darkness became intense, occasinal flashes of lightning and the rumble of thunder among the distant peaks added to the interest of the hour. About 9 P. M. we discovered lights ahead and we knew that we were approaching the hamlet of Santa Cruz, where we expected to overtake Moses and Aron with their train, and there we found them, comfortably swinging in their hammocks under the balcony of the chief house of the village, for in this country every home is open to the stranger. Both men were up in a moment and our mules quickly stripped of saddles and bridles were turned loose to graze, while the good lady of the house busied herself preparing a supper of tortillas and eggs, with the added luxury of "cafe con leche." Although the fare was plain and the service simple, I am sure a meal was never enjoyed more. Having disposed of everything in sight, we found our hammocks already swung, and fell into them with little ceremony and it is safe to say that costly couch never brought sweeter repose. So charmed were we with our first day's ride and first night's rest, that the writer determined to deliver a lecture on hammocks, but finding no opportunity, he wrote an article for the Indianapolis Journal which is clipped for this occasion. This was done several months after my

A SLIGHT INCLINE.

return from Honduras. In fact, I had been home long enough to forgets the discomforts of the trip, and only retained the pleasant features, and it is not reproduced here for any value it may possess in a scientific way, but simply to fill up, to ease the conscience of the writer and give him that comfortable feeling that one always has when they know they have given full measure even if the goods are below the standard.

ABOUT HAMMOCKS.

"Just now, while residents of the Northern States find themselves either trudging through wastes of snow or splashing through rivers of slush, seems a good time to take up the study of the hammock as a mild dissipation. Hanging in the corner there, is a relic of other days. True, it is slightly torn and somewhat stained by the storms and rough usage that are a part of camp life; still it recalls vividly the scenes among which it has swung—now on the mountain height, overlooking miles and miles of sunny landscape, now in deep gorges, echoing the wild music of some unnamed waterfall, now on the deck of some ocean racer, now on shore—always our inseparable companion and unfailing friend.

Probably a small proportion of the millions who daily recline in this restful contrivance have any idea of its origin. The name itself suggests a world of romance, and if we will trace its history we must leave the busy bustling times in which we live and go back through four centuries—back to the dreamy days of the Spanish conquest, days around which the purple mists of years have gathered, half concealing the actors in a sort of rosy haze—actors whose daring audacity and reckless bravery has never been excelled in the world's history, perhaps; back to the days of chivalry, when lovely ladies were most opportunely locked up in dismal towers to wait, sadly but hopefully, for the gallant knight in flashing armor who somehow always came to the rescue just in time to save the beautiful prisoner and carry her off as a slight reward for his timely service; back to the days of Columbus and his intrepid followers, for to this enterprising genius of the fifteenth century, mankind is indebted not only for the discovery of a new world, but for the invention of a new word, for he was the first to give it a place in the Spanish vocabulary by employing it in one of his glowing reports to his royal patrons, in which he describes the "hammaca" as one of the articles manufactured by the natives of the newly discovered islands, little dreaming that the rude "sleeping net" would force its way to the remotest corners of the earth, and the name would be pronounced by thousands who might never hear of its illustrious discoverer, for it is a fact that a large proportion of the inhabitants of tropical countries have never heard the name of the bold navigator of the Western seas.

It is uncertain whether the Indian word which the Spaniards adopted in the above form, referred to the article itself or the material from which it was made, or the manner of its use, or—who can deny it?—to the name of the inventor! One thing, however, is very certain: the Spaniards found it admirably adapted to their languid habits, and from them its use rapidly extended to other nations, until at the present time this delightful device is found in every land and is alike the solace of prince and peasant. In its restful meshes swing the high and the low, rich and poor, christian and pagan, old and young; in its enticing folds lovers are gently swayed to the music of their young dreams, or children, charmed into forgetfulness, slumber sweetly.

To the writer the name has a peculiar charm, and he never sees one without being carried back, as on invisible wings, to a certain island in the sunny sea, where for months it formed his only couch, and pictures of tropical luxuriance rise before him; again he hears the murmur of the wind among the palms, between which, in the distance, the blue sea is sparkling in the bright sunlight—memories of an endless round of summer days passed in most delicious idleness, in which to swing and dream was toil enough—a few brief months when he escaped the tyranny of the "barbarous pen" and ceased for a while to "scrawl strange words" for the "dregs of men"—a time when to read was wrong, to write was worse, and his whole business was to do nothing, simply to relax every muscle, rest every overtaxed nerve; to lie as one in a trance, with eyes half closed, giving up every sense to repose; to let fancy run wild and feel under no obligation to make prisoners of his thoughts for the amusement of some distant reader, who would not so much as thank one for the tiresome task; simply to live without a thought for the morrow, cooled by the fragrant breeze, lulled by the song of strange birds, or the low, rhythmic beat of the surf on the distant bar—every desire anticipated, every sense satisfied—a land of beauty, of sunshine, of contentment—land of fruits and flowers, of love and music—land of the hammock!

And so it happens that the simple invention that delights the world to-day had its origin in the brain of some unlettered savage, ages before Columbus was born; while yet the sovereigns of cultured Europe reclined on clumsy divans, or rested their royal persons in most uneasy chairs, these free sons of the forest where swinging in luxurious ease, rocked to sleep by the winds to the music of the restless waves that quarreled mildly with the coral reefs that lined the shore. But the "hammac" or "hammaca," as the Spaniards called it, was designed for utility first, pleasure afterwards, it was the outgrowth of necessity, for a country possessing every charm that the mind can conceive must needs have some opposing features, and these were found in this happy region in the form of poisonous insects of many varieties, including scorpions, centipedes, tarantulas and other equally interesting species, which could only be eluded by swinging clear of the earth. There is little doubt the idea was first suggested by the matted vines stretched from tree to tree, like great cables, over which the monkeys passed, or stopped to swing, the while screaming out a fierce challenge to some imaginary rival.

During our extended trip through the mountains of Guatemala and neighboring states the writer had many occasions to

DOWN GRADE.

thank the originator of the hammock for the security he enjoyed while traveling through a country overrun with insect pests, to say nothing of the serpents that were occasionally seen in the early light gliding away from the camp, to which they had been attracted by the enticing odors sent abroad by our native cook, no doubt—all of which would have rendered sleeping on the ground extremely disagreeable, if not dangerous. In these countries the hammock forms a necessary part of every traveler's outfit, and he might as well omit saddle, blankets, leggins and spurs, all of which he might possible get along without, but the hammock—never.

But do not take them with you when starting from the north, for the natives will only laugh at you for your trouble, and with good reason, for the pretty toys sold in the States would be of little value for actual service on a rough mountain journey, where the roads are but bridle paths, often leading through thorny thickets or between walls of rock barely wide enough for the passage of your mule, which offers the only means of transportation in those primitive countries. On the occasion referred to the writer and his companion had their hammocks made at the beginning of the overland journey by a native of wide experience in this line, and to his skill and thorough work we owed much during the months that followed. These swinging beds were made of heavy sail cloth strongly sewed, and were about twenty feet long and six feet wide in the middle, allowing the occupant to lie directly across, instead of lengthwise, thus assuring a degree of comfort impossible to attain in the narrow net with which most of us are familiar. The Mozos will hang these in five minutes and take them down in less time, rolling them up neatly with blankets enclosed, after which they are carefully strapped to the back of the saddles, and you are ready to move.

Delightful as the hammock is for an afternoon siesta, or a half hour's swing, it becomes very tiresome when occupied night after night for sleeping purposes, and if the writer of these reminiscences, would unflinchingly acknowledge the "truth, the whole truth, and nothing but the truth," he would tell you that one of the happiest hours of his life was when he beheld from the summit of a lofty pass the white walls of a city known to possess beds of good old-fashioned pattern. But the object of this paper is to remind the reader of the humble origin of the swing which he, or she, is enjoying at this very moment, rather than to call attention to its flaws or find fault with its construction, and whether it be the coarse net of the common sailor or the silken tangle of the prince, both should remember that the pleasure they may derive from its use is due to the intelligence of a dusky hero whose name and race have perished, but whose fame this article was written to perpetuate, for which honor alone, methinks, it were worth his while to have lived."

We stopped at Santa Cruz a few hours to look over a mining plant. A company of French capitalists, socalled had begun operations at this place about two years before our visit, and at enormous expense, erected mills for reducing the ore. Every modern contrivance had been introduced, all the ponderous machinery had been dragged over the mountains, months were occupied in the transportation of the powerful engines and massive boilers. At last everything was complete, and for a few weeks the village listened with astonishment to the thunder of the stamps and looked with awe upon the black cloud of smoke that hung over the busy place. Wonderful stories of wealth were carried back to France, and shares rose rapidly. When the last notch had been reached, it was discovered that the ore would not pay the expense of reduction, and the mine was suddenly abandoned. The managers of

NATIVE POTTERY, PICKED UP AT AGUA SALADA.

the scheme, who had been living like lords, at the expense of the distant stockholders, disappeared and the whole outfit was left to the mercy of the elements. Already the moss had begun to accumulate on the roof and the contemplative buzzard rested on the stack where lately sulphurous clouds arose. Inside we found the bats in possession. Instead of the busy hum of industry, our ears were assailed by the rustling wings of these dismal tenents, and the ominous croaking of frogs that swarmed in the waterway. It was a sad and touching sight. We knew that some innocent victims far away in sunny France had paid for all this folly. More than likely, hard working men and women, who in their anxiety to save a trifle for old age, had been lured into this investment by designing schemers, who had planned the failure before they left their native shores. There seems to be a wonderful fascination in far-away investments. Every day we find people sending to some distant dealer for goods that could be bought cheaper right at home, with every opportunity for examination. It is the element of uncertainty—the gambling instinct. Something great has been promised, and we will try a "chance," much as we go into lotteries and all manners of games that incur risk. There is an undeniable charm in the risk—as most of us know. But what have we to do with philosophy, with all the beauty of the tropical wilderness about us? Moses and Aaron and the train are miles ahead, we will follow: Each day is a repetition with a change of scene. Now toiling up the steep sides of mountains, now picking our way along the rocky bed of some mountain stream, now fording foaming torrents, here and there coming across the hut of a native squatter, and at long intervals passing through some little hamlet, stopping at night in the cabildos, or town house, which are always open to the traveler. These buildings are usually found on the central plaza and are regarded as common property. On arriving at a village, we immediately take possession of this public house, or such portions as are not already occupied. The Mozos swing the hammocks and build a fire on the earthern floor, then start on a canvass of the village for provisions, tortillas, frijoles, eggs, coffee, fruit, anything in fact that can be procured. To these supplies we added from our stock of tinned goods, and fared very well. When the various stores had been gathered in, Moses, who took the lead in such matters, would proceed to make the coffee, warm the tortillas and boil the eggs (providing they had been fortunate enough to secure any.) Meanwhile we spread our blankets around the cheerful blaze, that now illuminated the darkest corners of the windowless room. Supper over, we take a stroll around the village, stopping here and there to chat with the natives whom we found socially inclined and fond of gossip. Some of the young men and women were almost handsome. A few of the latter were very attractive indeed. Their very moderate costumes being arranged to display their charms to the best advantage. Their glossy black hair, carefully brushed, was sometimes loosely coiled but mostly hung in a luxuriant braid tied at the end with a bit of bright ribbon. They also knew how to place a rose or other flower to the best advantage, and were by no means ignorant of the arts of the modern coquet.

After sunset the inhabitants would be seen flitting from house to house, each carrying a blazing pine stick to light the way. The effect of these swiftly passing lights is striking and adds not a little to the picturesqueness of the scene. The interior of the dwellings are illuminated in the same manner and the writer has penned many a note and finished many a sketch, by the flickering light of these same knots.

In these primitive villages there are no rich or poor, no high or low, everyone owns some kind of a musical instrument, the guitar being the general favorite though accordians, harps and

MUD STOVE, VILLAGE OF PETOA.

violins are common, and among the pleasantest memories of this trip are those which recall the simple melodies of the native musicians. Their performance was doubtless crude, from an artistic standpoint, but I must confess, I have seldom heard anything more inspiring than some of those Spanish songs ringing out on the still night air, to the accompaniment of the harp or guitar. The language itself is musical and a certain touch of melancholly ran through them all that was very touching indeed.

About 9 o'clock we returned to the cabildo and sought our hammocks, where we would swing and smoke and tell yarns until one by one we gave way to the gentle influence of the drowsy god, and with our ears filled with the melody that comes faintly across the plaza, we glide imperceptable into the land of dreams.

Thus we continued on our way, making an average of five or six leagues in ten hours, sometimes stopping over a day or two to rest and sketch. We were always treated with the greatest kindness by the villagers. In some places we visited the native schools, in others we stopped to watch the women work on the panama hats, which require a great degree of skill in the weaving as well as in the preparation of the grass, which must be cut at a certain stage and cured by a certain method, which retains all the toughness and flexibility of the green product, but at the same time bleaches the long slim leaves to a snowy whiteness.

These hats have a world wide reputation and will last a life time. They are so closely woven that they will hold water and are so flexible that they can be tightly rolled and packed away for months without injury. They are sold at various prices, according to the quality of material used, and care put in the work. The cheapest we could find being $1.50 and from that up to $12.00.

The $1.50 hat requires a good solid week of constant work, while the finer grades will take from two to six weeks—we were told.

CHAPTER VIII.

A PLEASANT SURPRISE—COLINES AND A WEDDING—DRINK THE BRIDES HEALTH AND LOOSE OUR OWN—BEAUTIFUL DAYS ON THE ROAD—SANTA BARBARA—HOME OF THE PRESIDENT—LOSS OF MOSES AND AARON.

Perhaps no better description of this country could be given than that contained in the pages of our old memorandum book that has already been called into service so frequently—and as the sole object of this work is to describe scenery and incidents of travel in a primitive land, the reader will excuse the introduction of these rough notes.

"Pinélejo—9:30 P. M. After a ride of four hours we arrived at this place. Owing to the awful slowness of the Mozos (who evi-

EVENING BELLS.

dently had formed a strong attachment for some of the dusky beauties at La Pita) it was four o'clock before we left that hamlet. Scenery grand, much of the way through natural parks, the cactus now appeared in great variety, some beautiful flowering trees twenty feet in height. From the top of a mountain we had a magnificient view just as the sun was sinking; far below us the wide, rich plains stretched away for miles until finally walled in by distant ranges of mountains, piled one above another until the highest was lost among the clouds, but in all that wide expanse not a village was to be seen, not a cultivated field, not a sign of human activity. Often we ride for leagues along the "Camino Real" without seeing a hut or meeting a soul.

As usual Moses and Aaron had taken possession of the best house in the village and on our arrival we found supper waiting. An elegant meal lay on a white cloth with plates, knives and spoons! It was like a dream. We were astonished, and with good reason—but we were still more surprised, and pleased not a little when we learned that we we enjoying the hospitality of Dr. Bogran and family. The doctor is a brother of the President and one of the wealthiest and most influential citizens of the republic. We had been riding five whole days through his territory Aaron informed us. Mrs. Bogran and her charming daughters proved themselves royal entertainers and with music and mirth the evening passed all to swiftly. This gives an idea of the hearty wholesouled character of these people. They insisted that we should stop and rest a day, but we declined the kind invitation and parted with regret—on our part.

August 11.—About 3 P. M. we met a certain Senior Salvador Paredis, with whom my traveling companion had stopped on his last trip to the capitol, and, although on his way to Belize, he insisted that we should make his house our headquarters during our stay in the village, which was only about a league ahead. So it happens that we are again located in the largest and finest place in the town, Senor Salvador being a prosperous merchant and grower of coffee. When we approached this house I was somewhat surprised to see the mozos lead the mules in the front door. We followed without dismounting, and passed through a store room into a court yard where we were met by the Senora and several members of the family. They seemed genuinely glad to see us. At this place we saw for the first time the curassaw, or native wild turkey, in a state of domestication these handsome birds are almost as large as their northern cousins, and are greatly esteemed for the table, consequently the native hunters have almost exterminated them, and the bird is now rarely met with except in poultry yards, where it seems to feel perfectly at home.

Like most villages, this has no hotel but every house is open to the stranger. A boy is just now preparing coffee for our dinner. He has a large wooden block hollowed out like a mortar. In addition to that he is armed with a heavy pestle. With these crude tools he will shell out enough for two or three meals. From here we can see a number of coffee plantations on the slopes of the mountains.

August 12.—Just passed a train of 24 mules laden with coffee, two huge sacks to each beast, they were bound for San Pedro. This shipment was destined for the U. S. Market. Much the larger portion of the crop finds its way to England, France and Germany. The climate of Santa Barbara seems especially adapted to the successful cultivation of coffee, and the industry is rapidly extending. The coffee of this district enjoys so great a reputation in London that a very small proportion finds its way to the states; however an occassional consignment is shipped to New York by some intrepid trader, whose reward for his bravery is increased

reputation and profits, as this product rivals the finest Arabian beans; while experts declare its flavor to excel that of the best eastern brands.

One can hardly immagine a prettier sight than a well kept coffee plantation. The trees, which are planted in long straight rows, are carefully pruned to a height of about eight feet, thus enabling the pickers to reach the topmost branches from a low stool. The glossy leaves are bright green, the flowers white as snow, diffuse a delightful odor. Where the climate is favorable the trees yield their first crop the third year from planting, so that its cultivation offers a tempting field to investors, and it is not surprising that a large amount of American capital has been drawn this way. However, the largest proportion of these pioneers, have located in Nicaragua which offers better shipping facilities, if not a more stable government.

As the tree flowers from seven to nine months, the fruit ripens very unequally, for this reason the crop is gathered semi-annually, and in some cases, three times a year. If the tree is handsome when in full bloom it is no less so when covered with the deep crimson berries, which remind one somewhat of cherries, though they are larger and oblong, hanging in clusters.

The tree flourishes best at an elevation of 1000 to 4000 feet, with a moist climate, and an average temperature of about 70 degrees. These conditions prevail in this district, which is in fact the ideal coffee region of America. Only two things are necessary to the development of the industry in Honduras, the first is a government that will enjoy the confidence of prospective investors, the second, the completion of the long contemplated railroad from Puerto Cortez to the pacific, this would give a port on either coast, with better facilities for speedy transportation than are now, enjoyed by any of the smaller republics, and would insure a large and every way desirable class of emigrants.

August 13.—We found use for our "slickers" to-day, being caught in a sudden shower, but thanks to these huge water proof coats, we did not get wet. A slicker to be of use in a trip like this must be large enough to cover saddle, blankets and all. Ours answered every requirement. They are made of two thicknesses of heavy muslin, thoroughly saturated with fish oil, are of a bright yellow color and shine as though varnished. They are not fragrant, but turn water like glass.

August 14.—Have just stopped a few minutes to note a flock of buzzards that are so tame that one can approach within six feet before they will move, then they shamble off awkwardly, and if closely pursued will fly a few feet rising with considerable effort, giving a grunt of dissatisfaction. When they alight they have to run a few steps to get their balance. They are very clumsy on the ground, but once in the air their flight is most graceful. We often see large numbers at an immense height, describing huge circles, often disappearing in the clouds, then reappearing far above, mere black specks against the deep blue. It is against the law to shoot these birds. First offense $25.00 fine; second offense fine and imprisonment: third, death I presume, though I have no authority for the assumption; however, it is a righteous law, for if it were not for the services of these industrious animals the poor natives would have to bury their dead mules, cows etc., which would require an amount of exertion quite unbecoming a Honduranian.

August 15.—We are the guests of Senor Jose Galindo. His house consists of four poles set in the ground with a high sloping roof of palm leaves. The sides are open to allow ventilation. Jose is standing over in the corner talking to a woman. He is wrapped in an ugly stripped blanket and looks for all the world like an Egyptian Mummy revived. He don't know I am talking about him, if he did he would probably carve me into small bits with his huge machete, which he has just sharpened. While writing these lines a motherly old hen hopped from a beam overhead directly on my lap, where she rested a moment, calmly contemplating the scene, and doubtless deliberating as to her next move. These useful fowls are allowed the range of the house, as are

Native of the Interior—
Nervy but not dangerous.

all other domestic animals. Cows, calves, pigs, goats, ducks, geese and babies meet on terms of perfect equality. Even the dogs and cats are accorded no special advantages. Truly, a most democratic country, where even the beasts of the field enjoy equal privileges with the lord of the Manor.

August 16—To night finds us in a hut of different type—the interior of which presents a strange appearance. a single room with a couple of clumsily made chairs, a rough table and several hammocks, the floor of solid earth, no windows, all light being admitted through the narrow door, dark, gloomy and bad smeling. The inhabitants, are sallow complexioned, and sickly looking, altogether without enterprise. The women keep the world moving, doing all the work, carrying water and wood, gathering crops, cooking—everything in fact, while the men lie in their hammocks, smoking cigarettes, which they call on their wives or daughters to make, and the rolling of these fragrant cubes is one of the feminine duties."

Sometimes we met a funeral procession slowly toiling along the mountain trail; the corpse clad in the garments in which he died, was laid in a comfortable sort of a crate which was carried on the shoulders of four men, where it would roll from side to side, according to the inclination of the path; sometimes there were only four or five followers, who, as a rule, were as cheerful and contented as their dead comrade. They always had one or two musical instruments and as they picked their way slowly over the uncertain road, the melancholy wail of the violin started the echoes among the lonely ravines.

One evening we arrived at a small village, Colines, I think, just in time to attend a wedding. This was almost as hilarious an event as a funeral. It was quite dark, we had just finished our supper and were enjoying a smoke with our host, when our attention was attracted by strains of music, and a little later a procession came in view. Following the band, which consisted of a violin, an accordian, a guitar and picallo, came the men, after them, the ladies. All carried blazing knots. We joined the crowd and were soon at the Cabildo, a new building and quite pretentious. It was two stories in height, something rare, the upper part being set apart for municipal purposes, balls, etc. At one end of this large room was a raised platform, surrounded by a railing. As strangers we were quickly noted and the chief officer sent a messenger to invite us to come within the inclosure, where we were not only provided with seats, but enjoyed a good view of the contracting parties as well as the Alcalde and his subordinates. When the ladies were all seated, (the men standing outside the railing,) the Alcalde called for the doomed couple to come forth, and placing a chair beside the table they took their seats and at once became the center of attraction. The bride was short and fat and looked more like a stout Dutch girl than a Spanish beauty.

She was dressed in a light colored gown with many flounces, tucks, a wonderful quantity of lace, and a profusion of flowers. The groom made a better appearance with light pants, cut in the peculiar Spanish style and a close fitting roundabout of some dark material trimmed with velvet, with brass buttons brightly polished. He was a really handsome fellow and doubtless belonged to one of the "best families." At a signal from the Alcalde, one of the deputies read the marriage law, which occupied about twenty minutes time and impressed all present with the awful responsibility attending matrimonial ventures. The deputy having finished, the Alcalde arose and read a few lines from another book then holding up the rod of office, (a slim cane decorated with a bit of ribbon) put the terrible question to which the groom responded faintly, "I do," but looked as though he meant the opposite. He seemed thoroughly frightened. The same

CROSSING THE CHIMELECON.

question was put to the bride and her answer being satisfactory, the twain were declared to be one flesh. The couple were required to leave their autographs in a ponderous volume and the ceremony was over. To light this scene, the municipality furnished four candles, but only one bottle being available, three men were employed to hold them.

As blotting pads are unknown in this region, the signatures of the newly wedded were sanded by a deputy and the book closed. This was a civil marraige. The law requires all persons contemplating such a step to make known their designs by posting a notice in writing on the Cabildo at least twenty days in advance of the date fixed upon, then to come before the Alcalde and be married in public so there can never be any question raised in regard to the transaction. The church, however, does not recognize the civil process, therefore, it is necessary for those who wish to pose before the world in the wedded capacity, to be married by a priest, so in most instances the happy couple repair at once to the Padre and have the bans performed according to the cannons of the church, for which they usually add from twenty to fifty dollars to the treasury of the holy Father. For this information the writer is indebted to our host, who is presumed to know. For the civil service the charge is only twenty-five cents.

After the ceremony, the hall was cleared, the ladies being seated on benches on one side while the men stood against the opposite wall. As distinguished visitors, we were invited to retain our seats on the raised platform. From this exalted position we had a fine view of the hall. Presently the band struck up. An adventurous youth moved cautiously across the open space and bowing before a blushing damsel begged her hand for the first dance, which after a little maidenly hesitation she gave and the next moment the couple were whirling gracefully across the floor. This seemed to inspire two or three more timid spirits and soon the floor was filled with swiftly moving figures. The dim light of the flickering candles, the clouds of smoke, the gorgeous colors, red, blue, yellow, green and white, following each other in quick succession, as the merry throng swept up and down, in and out, back and forth, formed a picture, at once weird and facinating.

In the midst of the festivities the father of the bride sent a messenger to invite the strangers to join him in a "glass" to the health of the happy couple—this seemed an easy thing to do, and quite proper under the circumstances; crossing the hall we arrived before a table where the old fellow was busily engaged, fulfilling his mission as master of ceremonies, doing his duty heroically, and energetically too, drinking with every one whose phisical endurance was equal to the ordeal. After shaking hands he filled a huge bumper with a potion locally known as "Anasada," a frightful concoction of native rum and aniseed—Alas! that innocent unsuspecting strangers, should be thus imposed upon—liquid fire!—how it hissed and crackled as it burned its way slowly to the heels of our riding boots—talk of Jersey lightening it's like watered milk by comparison. Silently and sadly we sought our humble quarters—farewell blushing bride, goodby happy groom, adios—anasada.

As has already been stated, we usually arranged our days journey so as to be a few hours behind the train in order to enjoy the ride undisturbed by the clatter of the muleteers, whose constant altercation with their animals, while amusing for a time soon became monotonous to an exasperating degree.

The writer will not soon forget these rides, now over towering mountains, now across wide valleys, a new world on every hand—scarcely a familiar bird, tree or flower—everything new and strange, but beautiful and interesting nevertheless. Sometimes we rode for hours in silence, simply feasting our eyes on the scenery that changed in character every league as we approached the crest of the cordellires, that mighty range of mountains that extends without a break from Patagonia to Alaska—now our mules, ploded along sedately a half a mile above the clouds, that rolled below, like an ocean of silver. Here is the birth place of storms, and from our lofty position we could watch their formation, and note their progress as they swept along beneath us so close that the roar of wind and rain was distinctly audible, though the sun was shining brightly on these isolated peaks that rose above the mists like islands in a troubled sea. These riots of the elements occurred most frequently after midday; suddenly, and without apparent cause, a slight haze would be observed hanging over an elevated ravine, at first almost imperceptable, then more pronounced, until gradually trees and rocky bastions were hidden under a soft white blanket,—now the under portions assumed an ominous purplish hue and the shaddows grew denser every instant, until the opening of the ball was announced by a preliminary peal of thunder that echoed solemnly from crag to crag, startling the sluggish vulture from his gluttonous dreams—for he now appeared rising out of all this murky darkness, up—up—up into the clear blue ether, where he sailed slowly, majestically, a mile above the scene of commotion, a tiny mote in the infinite ocean of air—now the mutinous forces, directed by some unseen but noisy leader became more and more restless, the ever increasing masses of vapor, extend far over the valley, until the storm, breaking all bounds rushes across the plain, where consumed by its own passion, the cloud hosts soon disperse, leaving the world brighter and more beautiful than before. If we had our silent periods in these solitudes, they were followed by hours of social chatter, when conversion flowed steadily; what a variety of subjects were discussed on this three month's ride—old times, politics, religion, medicine, literature, art, agriculture. What strange experiences were recalled out of the dim past,—mysterious circumstances, spirit manifestations, rappings, sights and sounds—but above all what glorious freedom. Stopping when and where we choose, to lunch, or smoke, or read, or write, or simply to rest, lying on our backs, watching the mists wreathing themselves into a thousand fantastic forms about the rocky summits that towered on every hand, or noting the slowly moving shaddows as they followed each other across the vale until lost among the dark pine covered foot hills miles and miles away, and to feel that for once there was no hurry! If we did not reach our destination to-day, what matter, to-morrow would do. "Manana!" the word came to have a very enticing sound indeed.

THE LAST CANDLE STICK.

These mountains are the parents of a thousand crystal streams, and every time we came to one of these we found a valid excuse for stopping long enough to indulge in a bath. Occasionally we met a company of disappointed gold hunters returning to the states disgusted with the country, blind to its beauties, deaf to its music, dead to everything but the memory of their bitter failure. They expected to find mountains of gold—they found only barren rocks, and instead of returning like princes they must reappear among their friends with large patches on their pants. Of course the prospect of returning to the home of one's childhood under such circumstances is not exhilariting. We had tried it in our youth and from that day to this we have resolutely refused to search for wealth. It is a snare and a delusion.

Now and then we were overtaken by parties on their way to the mines. These fellows were full of hope, riding in hot haste, all impatience. We tried to make them understand there was no hurry, advised them to take their time—and a bath—once in a while—they needed it—told them the mountains of gold would not get away—in fact they were quite stationary and would wait patiently a whole year, a whole century for that matter, we did all we could to prolong their delusion, in fact we preached "Manana" to these hot headed rovers—advised them to travel slowly and enjoy themselves as they went a long, to save their strength as they would need it for the return trip, but our arguments were all in vain. They had no eyes, ears, hearts or minds for anything but gold, so they rushed on to find the coveted treasure securely locked in the mountains vaults—and the combination lost. And so it has been in "every age and clime" where one succeeds a thousand fail, so it will always be, for the simple reason that the success of one depends on the failure of another. Wherever you see a millionaire, you see a man, who through circumstances fortunate or otherwise, has been enabled to absorb the wealth produced by others. I say fortunate or otherwise advisedly because I'm not sure that wealth is a fortunate possession—but there's something mighty attractive about it.

But enough, this is the land of rest and romance, we have all we need to-day. The morrow takes care of itself. Away with trouble, away with cold philosophy! So we light our pipes and journey on, without a thought or care for the golden hoard that lies under our feet, perchance almost within our grasp. We arrive at Santa Barbara, a sleepy little town surrounded by mountains, 'dobe walls, red tiled roofs, projecting windows, huge old cathedral, large cabildo, narrow streets paved from wall to wall with cobble stones, women carrying water from the creek, some pretty, some not, but all straight and well formed; men laying in shade smoking, naked children playing in the plaza, native soldiers being drilled by an officer from Gautemala, wild set, ragged, barefooted, unkempt, wicked looking; drill with wooden sticks to represent guns, looks like childs play. This is the seat of government for the department of Santa Barbara, one of the most important towns in the republic from a political point of view. It is the home of President Bogran, whose family occupy the largest mansion in the city. It occupies a solid square on the Calle de La Constitution, and is furnished in a style of grandeur that astonishes the stranger, who has become accustomed to mud walls and earthern floors. As representatives of the United States government, we called at the mansion. The President was absent, being detained at the capitol by some diplomatic business, but Mrs. Bogran received us graciously and we spent a delightful half hour. Here we found beautiful rugs from the orient, books, paintings, statuary, in fact every evidence of wealth and culture. Our hostess called our attention particularly to a large collection of photos of the celebrated ruins of Coban, and explained them in charming Spanish. Her tones were low but very distinct and the language never sounded so musical as on this occasion. She is a native of Santa Barbara, but well educated and truly refined. The President was building a new residence on the mountain side just a thousand feet above the city. She was greatly interested in the new home and frequently rode up there to note progress. She thought they would spend their time between the two places, little dreaming that a few months later, the General, then the most popular man in the Republic, would be forced to flee for his life, seeking refuge in the United States.

Santa Barbara Broom 1891

In matters of dress, she followed the custom of the country, her gown of silk was plainly made and over her shoulders was thrown, with careless grace, a richly embroidered shawl, while her hair neatly braided was allowed to hang over her shoulders.

The principal industries here are the manufacture of native pottery, dobe blocks, or bricks, being huge square blocks of earth mixed with grass and dried in the sun. These, when built in a four foot wall with mud for mortar, will last for ages in this frostless climate. The women are also largely engaged in the manufacture of panama hats and cigars, the latter the vilest we have met.

As there was no hotel in the city, we rented a whole house, facing the Calle de Libertad, one of the aristocratic streets, our new residence consisted of one room. Here Aaron swung our hammocks and in five minutes we were as much at home as though we had always lived there. Back of our mansion was a garden surrounded by a high stone wall capped with red tile, this was over grown with vines and had the appearance of being very ancient. It was a favorite resort for the buzzards, and it was nothing unusual, after a shower, to see twenty-five or thirty perched on this wall with their wings out-spread drying in the sun.

The former owner of this property must have been a man of rare taste for in the center of this flowery retreat is a summer house of rustic pattern provided with comfortable seats. From this place we caught a glimpse of the church with its tall white dome. showing through an opening in the trees. It was very pleasant to sit there, breathing the perfumed air and listening to the sounds of the street that came so faintly—the bugle call from the Cabildo, the clatter of mules over the cobble stone, the drum, or the military band. In fact we found it much pleasanter to sit out there and smoke those dainty Spanish cigarettes than to work, especially when our friend, Don Funas' pretty daughter rolled them so prettily and insisted so sweetly that we test the product of her genius. But we could not tarry always, though to tell the truth, none of us were anxious to mount the mules, for we knew that the road was rougher than ever, and it would be a long time before we could find as pleasant a resting place. While here, one of our animals was bitten by a tarantula, or horse spider. The poor creature lived only a few hours. Some time was lost hunting up another to take its place. However, Moses persuaded a poor native that sixty pesos (dollars) were much more to be desired than an old gray mule and so our ranks were filled. Then occured one of those exasperating circumstances that sometimes mar the pleasure of travel in this county—the owner of a pasture lot, a wily rascal, had agreed for a certain stipulated sum to allow our mules to graze therein, but when Moses and Aaron appeared with the amount, he thought he saw an opportunity to bleed the "gringos" and to that end, demanded just twice the sum agreed upon and purposed to hold the stock until the demand was met. This was a condition of affairs that delighted our Olancho men. Moses calmly covered the old sinner with a gun, while Aaron brought out the mules. Then throwing down the price agreed upon he left the Don swearing vengance, which soon followed. Just as we were ready to start a body of soldiers surrounded our faithful servants, who were marched off to the Cabildo to answer to the charge of highway robbery. The Alcalde seemed a decent fellow and when the matter was explained, he dismissed the case at once and threatened to have the extortioner placed in the stocks. Moses and Aaron were promptly released but their proud spirits could not bear the humiliation and although fully vindicated, they refused resolutely to go another mile. They had been paid a months wages in advance, this they returned and set their faces toward the wilds of Olancho. Santa Barbara was entirely too refined for these children of the mountains. They could not brook the cold conventionalities of this highly civilized community. So we were forced to say good bye, and we watched them start on their little jaunt of a hundred miles with real regret. Each one carried his hammock and blanket neatly rolled and slung over the shoulder by a stout leather strap. Their machetes newly ground flashed in the sun; their huge revolvers were freshly charged, and we knew that any differences that might arise between these men and the villagers, on their return trip, would be swiftly adjusted, according to the laws of justice as understood by these simple-minded children of the forest.

BOUND FOR THE MIRES.

This change of affairs caused another delay, but really there was no particular hurry and one more day in the romantic little city was not considered in the light of a misfortune. Santiago was particularly well pleased, as his affections had been quite won by a certain black-eyed damsel whose residence, fronting on the

Calle de la Paz, was provided with a large projecting window, the iron bars of which had been accidently or otherwise pressed apart sufficiently to admit the arm of the lover. Here the young man had spent many happy evenings in the deep shadow of the wide projecting roof. The words spoken were few, and whispered, for should the old Don learn of these meetings, good bye happy dreams. Thanks to the bent bars, he could reach through the opening and clasp the object of his devotion with one arm, and so, silently, but not less stoutly, Cupid forged the chains that seemed like bonds of silk, but which later on may gall the poor victims beyond endurance—but why anticipate, while the world stands, maids will charm, lovers will woo, both blind and deaf to every object but one—wealth, position, high asperations, all will be sacrificed on the rose strewn altar of the smiling tyrant, and perhaps it's best. Cold calculation usually makes even greater blunders. Marriages of convenience often prove very inconvenient indeed.

Meanwhile what havoc these rustic beauties are causing among the poor defenceless youths of the little republic! How destinies are shaped by a glimpse of a shining braid, the glance of eye quickly lowered, the tell tale blush—what magnetic power lurks in those dark, lustrous orbs, in whose depths are reflected just enough of melancholy to arrouse interest—then sympathy—then—fatal step—love!

The climate of Honduras, especially the elevated plateaus is simply superb, here, at an elevation of from 2,500 to 3,000 feet above the sea nothing could be more charming—to exaggerate the beauty of the scenery or the seasons would seem impossible—"like our June" comes as near telling the story as words will do it—yet it lacks a great deal—for in Indiana, June cannot be fully depended upon—there will be some excessively hot days, others uncomfortably cool—there will be days without a ghost of a zepher, when one would almost give all they possess for a good full breath of fresh air.

This is not the case in Honduras, (and the same is true of the higher portions of Guatemala and Nicaragua) where the temperature is uniform, very seldom rising above 85 degrees at noon, in the shade—and falling at night to 65 degrees, making blankets a necessity. During the day a delightful breeze prevails, it comes pure and clear as crystal, from the great Pacific ocean, washed clean by its long tussell with the salt water—to breath it means new life and hope to the invalid, and fills the heart of the strong with joy.

In this almost perfect climate nearly every fruit and flower can be successfully cultivated, yet very little attention is paid to either agriculture or floriculture by the contented natives, who prefer to subsist on the cattle that range the heights, free as the air, or the the unfettered streams.

No doubt some one has a legal claim on each and all of these wanderers, but if such is the case, the innocent souls who inhabitate this terrestial paradise, seem quite ignorant of the fact, so it came to pass that we were often regaled on fresh veal or pork as the case might be, by these free-handed sons of the mountain, whose fleet footed ponies and fateful lassoes, proved the undoing of many a sleek calf or yearling, when the demands of hospitality called for the sacrifice—with a wild whoop the boys set off down the valley where the rich grass, revived by the recent rains attract the droves from the higher slopes. They ride at reckless speed, with saddle or without, the herd, panic stricken by the swift descent and demoniac yells, scatter in every direction, thus enabling their pursuers to select the very finest young steer; then begins a race for life—screaming like madmen, the daring riders urge their wiry little beasts to their utmost speed—away they go with the fleetness of the wind, rocks and hidden gullies are cleared at a bound, for these wild cattle are little inferior to the red deer in the matter of swiftness and high jumping—but it's only a matter of time—the tough little ponies are gradually, but surely gaining on the quarry, the riders, encouraged, renew their yells as they swing the lariats preparatory to the fatal throw—a little closer—now!—swish! they fly straight and swift as arrows, landing squarely over the horns—instantly the horse throws himself on his haunches—if horse and rider were one the movement could not be more timely—in an instant the animal is on its knees—almost similtaneously another lasso is thrown from the opposite side, and while the obedient horses hold the line taut the hunters dispatch the game—in less time than it takes to tell it the steer is transformed into a dressed beef—the hide is carefully preserved, all the meat that can be used at once is brought home, the remainder being "jerked" or dried in the sun, thus preserving it for some future emergency when the fresh article may not be so readily obtained.

CHAPTER IX.

FROM SANTA BARBARA TO THE CAPITOL, WITH SOME DIGRESSIONS.

From this time we were to be led by angels, two having been discovered in the persons of Don Pedro Angeles and his son Bartholomew, who had for the trifling consideration of fourteen dollars a month and Tortillas, consented to fill the position lately vacated by the faithful Olanchans.

Though unprovided with the conventional wings and arrayed in the simple style of the country, our new guides proved efficient and trustworthy.

Finally, everything having been satisfactorily adjusted and "Adois" repeated, we rode away accompanied by a delegation of our newly made acquaintances, for such is the the custom of the country. These good fellows followed us about two leagues, then, with much hand shaking and drinking of each others health, we parted.

In Honduras, the host always rides out six, eight or ten miles to meet the coming guest, his saddle bags well supplied with refreshments adapted to this peculiar climate, and considered quite essential on such occasions. If the approaching visitor be a man of great importance, he will be met by a large party, and the chances are that he will need some friendly assistance before he arrives at his destination. When he departs, the same party will escort him to the nearest village where the ordeal of parting must be gone through, which is sometimes painfully prolonged.

Three days later our train was wending its way through the narrow streets of Comayagua, the old Spanish capitol. Here we found a hotel and enjoyed the luxury of beds, a large room with double doors opening on the street, meals served on a table with the preliminary bowl of soup, and best of all, "Pan Blanco." Yes, real loaves of white bread, fresh vension—and ants.

Looking over that old memorandum book once more, I find the following :

"September 1.—Comfortable hotel—good room—good bed—wonderful table. This morning when I broke my little loaf of white bread (think of it! actually white bread) and five thousand ants began marching out in good order, I was surprised—felt I was imposing on the landlady by accepting so much without making some remuneration. Mentioned the subject, but the good woman declared I need feel under no obligations as they were furnished with the bread, consequently cost her nothing. I was satisfied so far as the hostess was concerned, but conscience still troubled me—felt that it was wrong to eat these innocent and unsuspecting insects, when they had given no cause for offense, but where simply roaming around the fragrant caverns of the Pan Blanco in ignorance of the awful fate awaiting them. It wasn't that I objected to ants as an article of diet, or that I was prejudiced against them in any way, but felt it was taking a mean advantage to spring upon them in this unfeeling manner. Influenced by these arguments, the Senora divided the loaf in four pieces, tapping them briskly on the table. The surprised tenants came trooping out of every crevice, distributing themselves over the cloth. She then handed me the pieces with a satisfied smile remarking that they now had fair warning, and if any failed to escape it would be no fault of mine. She admired the disposition I had shown and hoped Senor would now rest quite easy."

LA MERCED.

Ants are everywhere in Central America, at all altitudes from the coast to the summit of the highest mountain, large, small, medium and betweens. Some fierce and agressive, not waiting to be attacted, but rushing madly to the fray, others timid and shy, taking alarm at the slightest sound, falling into your soup or coffee in their wild flight.

How we reveled among all these luxuries—and were half minded to stop indifinitely!

About noon on the day of our arrival we were aroused from our reveries by the sound of an approaching band accompanied by the clatter of a numerous squad of riders. We soon learned the cause of all this commotion. A company of strolling acrobats were just now advertising a performance for the evening. One of the actors, arrayed as a clown, was seated backwards on an old gray mule, as he passed he smiled and bowed to the ladies, but shook his fists at the small boys, who yelled without ceasing. Arriving before our house he stopped and announced in a loud voice, that there would be a circus in the evening in a certain house, in a certain street, at a certarn hour, where all sorts of performances possible and impossible were to be enacted. Among the attractions was the inevitable "human ostrich," who would swallow a collection of knives, forks and nails, completing the meal by consuming a quart of broken glass, the same to be prepared by some member of the audience. A circus in Honduras is worth seeing, so, when the hour arrived we started out guided by the sound of music and a confused babel of voices in the direction of the plaza. The night was beautiful, the full moon flooded the deserted streets with a soft mellow light, the long rows of houses tightly closed stretched away in the dim distance. Here and there we passed the crumbling ruins of some old time church, now overgrown with ivy, the home of owls and bats. These ancient towers with their dismal tenants wear a strangely spectral look looming up through the silvery mist that gathers over the plain at night fall. We found the place at last, a very narrow street under the shadow of the great cathedral. A motley crowd had already gathered. Men, woman and chilnren in all stages of dress and undress. As usual the youngsters were quite free of clothing, while those a little farther advanced wore short shirts alone- The big boys, however, appeared in full evening costume, consisting of drawers and shirt, broad sombreros and cigarettes. These latter, strutted around like turkey cocks hunching the smaller fry right and left after the manner of young snobs of similar caliber everywhere. Three ragged soldiers with real guns, guarded the arched entrance, over which hung an oil lamp that gave out a little light and a great deal of smoke. On depositing a couple of *reals* in the hand of one of the guards, we were allowed to enter. Passing through a long dark hall we came out in a court, where a trapeze and bar had been erected, and a band was industriously punishing a half dozen instruments, which in turn screamed back a wild but useless protest. The drum fairly roared with rage, but a battered brass horn seemed to suffer most, if one might judge by the agonizing shrieks with which it rent the still air of night.

The place filled rapidly, for if there is anything these people love it is noise and smoke. The flickering light from the torches, the strange faces and costumes and rainbow array of colors, produced an effect at once novel and wierd. The performance proved very tame, as usual the "ostrich" was unable to carry out his part of the program, owing to a painful accident caused by swallowing a butchers saw, a circumstance greatly regretted by the managers who begged the kind indulgence of the audience, etc. We were soon glad to escape to the clearer air of the street, which was now almost empty. Here we found an old woman diligently engaged in the manufacture of milk punch. Before her was a little fire of pine wood, on one side a supply of sticks, with which to replenish it, on the other, a large wooden tray containing several bottles of native rum, a pan full of eggs, a little box of cinnamon, a jug of milk, some sugar in a broken dish. In the midst of the fire stood an earthern vessel filled with milk which was kept at the boiling point. Business was not pressing—the dealer seemed very poor—moreover the punch diffused a most enticing aroma—her price was moderate—only a media—($6\frac{1}{4}$ cents)—would we try her goods? but no, visions of Colines, and the wedding, with the "Anasada" incident came before us. We would take no risks, so calling up the three ragamuffins who still stood guard, although there was no further necessity for their services, we invited them to try the compound, then calmly waited to see them drop, but were dissappointed. Indeed they seemed to enjoy the experiment and expressed their gratitude by many low bows, and muttered "gracias, senor, muches gracias," even offering to repeat the act if "Senor" desired.

The following letter from the Pittsburgh Dispatch, will give a pretty good idea of this old town and is therefore inserted without apology.

"A charming old Spanish town, lying asleep in the warm sunlight, surrounded by groves of orange trees, whose odorous blossoms fill the air with a delicate perfume all the year through, for here spring, summer, autumn and winter are merged in one deligtful season, and while the ripe fruit glistens like gold among the deep green foliage of one tree its neighbor will be found in full bloom.

Years ago this was the most populous and prosperous city in

Honduras, having, it is alleged, not less than 30,000 inhabitants, but since the removal of the capitol to Tegucigalpa the place has been steadily retrograding until, at the present time, the population does not exceed 6,000.

The long narrow streets stretch away in dim perspective, lined with rows of one story adobe houses, many of them deserted and in ruins. A dozen or more old churches, their roofless walls overgrown with moss and vines, attest the religious fervor of the people in those old, happy days, when the markets were thronged with eager buyers from a hundred interior villages, and the plaza echoed the confused sounds of music and barter, the jargon of tradesmen and disputing muleteers. Now the great square is forsaken, the vast cathedral with its massive towers and lofty dome seems a magnificient monument erected over a dead and buried community; its glowing white walls rising high above the adjacent buildings are visible for miles, a sure guide to the solitary traveler on the plain. I prefer it as it is to-day, with its drowsy atmosphere, its half heard sounds, the far away musical hum of bees, flitting from flower to flower in the white walled garden.

Here we lay down life's burden and rest awhile from the consuming cares that pursue us in more civilized lands. The artificial desires that counterbalance the pleasures of cultured society are here unknown. Senora Maria is not dying of envy because Senora La Paz's new bonnet is a day later than her own from Paris; in fact, Senora Maria does not give Senora La Paz's headgear a thought, and, to tell the truth, neither of these ladies possess such an article, probably never saw one. She wears

a broad rimmed straw hat, just like her good husband's, and is quite satisfied therewith.

Here is no distracting shreik of locomotives, no horrid din of contending cabmen, no roar of traffic.

Comayagua is built in the midst of the plain of the same name, having an elevation, of about 2,000 feet above the sea; consequently enjoys a climate that is unsurpassed. The air is wonderfully pure and exhilarating, the scenery grand. The broad valley stretches away for leagues, a natural park, the surface gently undulating, watered by numerous streams, dotted with clumps of hardy oaks, giant cactus, tree ferns, with isolated piles of rock over run with flowering vines. Over all tower the mountains, vast, dim, cloudcrowned. These rise on every side to a height of 5,000 to 7,000 feet ilke grim sentinels guarding the lovely plain—on their elevated slopes every fruit and vegetable known to the temperate zone may be grown successfully. Pears, peaches and plums flourish, beside oranges, bananas and mangos, while corn, wheat and oats are cultivated in connection with upland rice, coffee and cacao. In the markets we find tomatoes, cabbage, potatoes, not equal to those produced in the states, but very fair, indeed, when we consider the crude manner of cultivation. With modern implements and methods, wonderful results might be realized.

The town is not dead—only sleeping. Some day it will awaken to the grand possibilities within its reach. A railroad will be built from San Pedro, making her vast resources available, the toil and discontent of a higher civilization will overcome the happy dwellers in this quiet vale. Vain ambitions, envy, hatred but half concealed, in fact all the evils of an "educated and refined" community will be upon them. However, this catastrophe is not eminent. The Hondurians cannot be hurried; no force of oratory or elegance of speech can move them beyond their natural gait; in all their movements they are slow, sedate, stately—haste is undignified. "Crazy as a Frenchman" is the usual appelation applied to Americans who insist on pushing their schemes with reckless promptitude.

You may not be sure of your breakfast, dinner or tea, here, but one thing you can always depend on, that is bright, sunshiny weather; dark, dull, rainy days are unknown. Occasionally a thunder storm sweeps over the plain obscuring the sky for a quarter, sometimes a half hour; these usually occur from 4 to 5 o'clock in the afternoon. Coming as they do at the warmest hour of the day, these swiftly passing showers are most refreshing, for a few minutes the rain falls in torrents washing the cobbled streets till they are as white as grandmothers kitchen floor after its tri-weekly scrubbing—then follows the daily marvel, a tropical sunset—the lead colored clouds that lately trailed their gray skirts across the fields, are scattered now. The sun hanging over the western rim of this vast basin floods the valley with golden light, straggling forms of vapor linger here and there, or cling about the isolated peaks, whence they stream out like banners from lofty battlements, reflecting every shifting tint of the evening sky—now the distant precipices glow like burnished gold—now they fade gradually to pale crimson, only to be swallowed up a moment latter by the deep purple shadows that fall over the world like the soft sil-

ken curtains drawn about the cradle of the sleeping prince—but this twilight is of short duration to-night—for the full moon is rising, slowly, her face, shining like a silver shield—now we trace the black outline of rock and tree against that perfect arc of light—then swinging clear of all earthly obstructions, she sails majestically through through the sky, queen of the tropical night—filling the streets with a mild yet beautiful radience unknown in higher latitudes.

Comayagua is one of those favored towns possessing a hotel—the "Americano." Here you can have the native tortillas, with their inseparable companion dish frijoles, coffee, milk, venison or pork, eggs and vegetables, a large airy room, all at an expense of

$1.50 a day in this currency, equal to about 90 cents in gold. A delightful retreat from the cold blasts of winter or the fierce heat of summer, for here the thermoneter rarely marks a higher temperature than 85 degrees during the warmest season, or lower than 75 degrees in winter—a land of perpetual spring, of flowers, birds, music, sunlight.

This town ought to command the respect of the traveler for its age, if for nothing else. In a country where everything is new, a city dating back to 1540 deserves the title of ancient—only forty-eight years after Columbus first sighted the lofty peak of Conger Hoy, Alonzo Casceras a Lieutenant of Cortez, acting under the instruction of that general, proceeded to Honduras with an army of one thousand men for the purpose of selecting a site for a city, which Corteq directed him to build as nearly as possible at a point half way between the oceans. So closely did he follow his instructions that it is said the exact center is less than four miles north of the plaza, which seems the more remarkable when we consider that no measurements were made.

Scarcely a building in the city but has suffered more or less from revolutions and earthquakes, but the former have been vastly the more destructive. All the churches bear the marks of musket or cannon balls, and a large number have been quite destroyed. Private residences also show where the battle raged. On one of the main streets we noticed the iron bars that protect the projecting windows, were often broken and twisted in all manner of shapes. We could not imagine what force could have been used to effect such ruin, but on making inquiry were told that it was done by the cannons of an attacking party who had placed an old fiield piece at the end of the street and amused themselves by practicing on the cathedral, which loomed up at the opposite end. The fire was not well directed and some balls bounced along the cobble stones or glanced up through these barred windows. Many conspirators have been executed here from time to time, probably the last being General Delgrado and four companions, who were shot in front of the ancient church of La Merced in November, 1886. It is reported that President Bogran was anxious to save the General's life but was prevented by the obstinacy of the old soldier, who preferred to die rather than to live through the mercy of his hated rival. However, his last request was granted, which was that he might be allowed to give the command to fire, and at the proper moment his voice rang out clear and loud, and he fell, dying almost before the echoes had ceased to vibrate among the tottering towers of the old church.

Here we met Jack Humphrey, an adventurer, originally from Connecticut, but whose home was anywhere; the son of wealthy parents, he had started in life with the brightest prospects thoroughly educated and possessing natural ability of a high order, he might have made his mark in any community, but he had the misfortune to fall in love at an early age with a girl, who, after an engagement of a year, suddenly changed her mind, in other words another fellow proved more attractive and Jack was thrown over. From that day he became a wanderer, roving from place to place with no other object than to put in his time and exist at the expense of others, and find what amusement he could as he went along. He was a pleasant fellow and knew a little of everything and was cheerful with all—rain or shine, hot or cold—it was all the same to Jack. He was one of those odd characters that are occasionally met in these out of way places. No doubt he would long since have been forgotten had it not been for the amusement he afforded us one time several weeks later. We had left him peacefully smoking on the steps of the hotel, when we rode out of Comayagua, never expecting to see him again; finding we had plenty of time and not having quite as much mountian experience as we desired, we decided to take an excursion to a town celebrated for the excellence of its cigars. The following quotation from a letter printed in the Indianapolis Journal will describe our next meeting and incidently give the reader a glimpse into a home life of a native cabinet maker and undertaker.

"Santa Rosa is an Indian peublo, consisting of a few dozen huts, hid away among the mountains of Honduras. It has little to interest the traveler and we were heartily tired of it; we had been waiting nearly a week for Santiago to bring in our two most valuable mules, which, thanks to the lazy Indian's carelessness, had strayed in the bush. Time dragged heavilly. We had literally devoured our only newspaper, now three months old—"local brevities," "news items," "funnygraphs." advertisemens, and finally in our desperation, the editorials themselves—and there is no telling what the result would have been but for the opertune arrival of Jack Humphrey, whom we had left weeks ago in the sleepy town of Comayagua. It is hardly necessary to say that we were delighted to see the good natured vagabond once more. He was mounted on his old white mule, followed by his Indian servant. Jack was a typical Yankee, whose aimless wanderings had at last landed him in Honduras where fortune seemed to have utterly forsaken him. But his was a cheerful soul never giving up to despair. His resources were endless, his wit inexhaustable; he could mend a clock, write a sermon, shoe a horse, lecture on law or medicine. Poetry trickled from his pen like drops from a melting icicle. He could paint a house or portrait with equal facility, and as for scenes and signs, he could do them blindfolded, so he said. He taught boxing one season and the next traveled as a professor of music. He did everything in

fact, but work, and saved everything but money. The collection of curios, which he packed about from camp to camp, would have made a respectable start for a museum.

Such a restless spirit could not exist long without some distraction, and he began at once to look around for amusement. Right across the street was the shop and residence of Jose Funeralo, the undertaker. His establishment was not extensive, but it abounded in interesting features. The business occupied the entire block, which consisted of one house containing a single room about twelve by twenty feet. One corner was devoted to the culinary department, with its stone fire place, another was used as a general store house for all the odds and ends required by the native housewife—a half dozen earthern vessels, heaps of tattered blankets, well worn hammocks, and over all this wreckage, a picture of the Pope. As a further precaution against evil influences, the good man had nailed to the wall in the remaining space, a rude cross of his own carving. Among these picturesque surroundings, Don Jose carried on his trade; his tools were few and simple—a saw, a hatchet, a square, a glue pot, that was seldom used, with the usual rubish that accumulates on the bench of a wood worker. The plant was not large, but it was quite as extensive as the trade demanded. Times were dull, and our swarthy neighbor seemed quite content to repose on the half finished coffin, dreamily speculating as to who would be its occupant, hoping it might be one of the wealthy Dons, perhaps, but all the time smoking serenely, while Madame prepared the tortillas, with infinite toil, for her lord's supper.

Jack saw his opportunity and soon had Jose convinced that all he needed was a big "bargain" sign. As the natives could neither read nor write, it was decided to have it lettered in English, with the view of catching the "transient custom," as Jack explained, of travelers who were constantly coming and going from the mines. You can judge of the astonishment with which we read the announcement next day. It was on white muslin, two yards wide, stretched across the entire front, lettered in bright red as follows:

"*Jose Funeralo, Undertaker, begs to inform the public that he is now prepared to handle all first-class corpses with neatness and dispatch. His long experience enables him to guarantee satisfaction and he is willing to enter into an agreement with prospective customers by which he will become personally responsible for any uprising or riotous behavior on the part of those instrusted to his care. He points with pride to the long list of persons he has buried in the years that are gone, not one of whom has ever complained or found fault with coffin or trimming.*

SPECIAL OFFER: In order to secure desirable subjects during the next thirty days, only, I will allow a discount of fifty per cent. and six months credit, and all persons who contemplate dying in the near future should take advantage of this golden opportuniy and die now. Grand Saturday Matinee! Ladies and children half price."

The sign was a tremendous success, attracting as much attention from the Indians who could not read as from the travelers who could. The shop suddenly became the center of attraction. Jose was delighted. The miners "caught on" and ordered coffins of all sizes by the dozen, coffins for individuals, for whole families, coffins for themselves, for their friends, for Christmas gifts, for wedding presents, all to be delivered within the time limit.

All went well until the Padre, from Santa Barbara, arrived one day to hear confessions and receive contributions. He read the flaming announcement with considerable emotion and immediately ordered it pulled down, after which he translated the words to the frightened director of funerals. This the secret of Jack's sudden call to a new field of labor.

The childlike simplicity of these people is such that they are continually imposed on by every fakir that comes along. This incident, which is true, names excepted, is only one of many similar in character, witnessed by the writer during his sojourn in this land of sunshine and hammocks."

From Comayagua we advanced on Tegucigalpa, the road for the most part being broad and graded. This highway had been constructed at great expense about two years before our visit, and is a lasting monument to the enterprise of Gen. Bogran, under whose administration the work was performed. A similar road has been constructed from the Capital to the Pacific Coast, thus cutting down the time between those points from five or six days to about forty-eight hours for riders, or sixty hours for packs. The road is badly damaged in some places by washouts, in others by slides, which occur during the wet season. There seems no excuse for this neglect, when we remember the soldiers that are maintained in absolute idleness at the government's expense, and we would suggest to the executive, whoever he may be at this time, that they turn those ragged hordes on the roads in sufficient numbers to keep them in repair. This is only a suggestion and no bill will be rendered for the advice, and no offense will be taken if it is not adopted, nevertheless if we were running that country, we would see to it that these fellows had something to do beside drilling with painted sticks a short half hour each day.

We left this highway once to look over some deserted mines. They lay a few leagues to the north in a region celebrated for its scenery, and remote from traveled paths. The plant if it might be so termed, had been abandoned more than a hundred years ago on account of certain strange sights and sounds that could not be explained, and consequently were taken as a delicate hint that his Satanic majesty considered the advance of the workmen in the light of an invasion of his domain. There were rumbling sounds in the depths of the earth, strange lights appeared at night, smoke rose from the ground without apparent cause; in the dark recesses frightful apparitions were seen, their eyes like balls of fire, their bodies encircled by pale blue flames; miners dissappeared and it was believed that they were carried off bodily and cast into the pit—the bottomless pit, there to be tormented with visions of golden nuggets, which they could never touch, but for which they

would struggle, fight, weep, or rave forever—forever and aye—such was the fate we were told, of those who dared to enter this forbidden vale. No wonder those old Spaniards deserted the claim. Most anyone would have done so; if only one half that was told was true, it would be enough to discourage the boldest gold hunter. Still it was hard to give up the richest mine in the world, for here, according to tradition, they took out blocks of virgin gold weighing hundreds of pounds. Such were the stories concerning the fabled spot, all of which were firmly believed by the simple folk who inhabit these remote valleys, and any attempt to penetrate the mystery surrounding the location of the lost eldorado was discouraged by all the power of native eloquence—and many tales were told of the sudden disappearance of reckless adventurers who persisted in pursuing their investigations in the face of all their warnings.

Nevertheless, we decided to go over there and see if the same influence still prevailed, if not we would bring back a few hundred weight of the metal. But for some reason we were unable to locate the Bonanza, and after searching over a wide territory we were forced to the conclusion that the legends were quite true, and that the Prince of Darkness had actually carried off the whole oufit, or hidden it so safely as to defy all attempts to discover the secret. We thought we had it once. There was a bright gleam of shining metal on the side of a mountain, it reflected the sun like a mirror. Yes, there it was, a thick seam of pure gold a hundred feet long. There was no mistake about it. With a field glass we could plainly see and follow the gilded line which had been exposed by a recent landslide. It must be at least six feet thick, the rock above and below appeared to be be composed of grey sandstone seamed with purple colored quartz. Untold millions were in sight, almost within our grasp, all we had to do was to cross a deep ravine, climb the side of a hill and chop out as much as we wished. Four or five hours hard struggle found us at the foot of the the cliff, it was much higher than it seemed at a distance, but we were not deceived, we could see it clearly now, the seam was even thicker than it appeared when first noted. We were now directly under it and some places the the rock wall projected over our heads. It was about forty feet above where we stood. All sense of fatigue left us, everything was forgotten but the one gigantic fact—that we were millionaires, and best of all not a soul knew our secret. We had undertaken this excursion alone, it was all our own. We sat down and made some calculations. There was no doubt hundreds of tons of gold in sight; to even estimate its value was out of question. We would just call it a hundred million a piece then someone else might have what was left, while we were getting our breath we invested our fortune, so much in government securities, so much in real estate, so much in this, so much in that, then we counted up our income. We were very modest, conservative in fact, we decided to be satisfied with 3 per cent. net—what would that amount to? this was an interesting problem and we worked it out on the smooth face of the cliff, $3,000,000 a year! T-h-r-e-e M-i-l-l-i-o-n D-o-l-l-a-r-s—My heart stood still,—I lived in sort of trance; the figures were too vast—they conveyed no meaning to my dazed intelect—I tried to divide the sum in order to comprehend my good fortune, but found myself too weak and confused by the tremendous revelation to make the attempt, my brain was in a whirl, I seemed floating through space, attended by a train of livered slaves, who anticipated every desire. Palaces loomed up through the golden mists—beautiful parks stretched in lovely perspective, with groups of statuary and shimmering fountains, There were vast libraries, and galleries, stored with the art treasures of a dozen centuries—and all my own! How I pitied my poor old neighbors back in the states who were struggling along with only a few hundred thousands to their credit.

My companion was not affected to the same extent, he realized we had a good thing and was reasonably glad, but being a practical business man, he did not loose his head; he thought by living in a frugal way, and watching all the little expenses, we might get along nicely and add a comfortable sum to the principal each year,—he said we must be careful and conservative in the matter of investments. We then figured to learn as near as possible what our daily income would be and were somewhat alarmed when we learned that it would not exceed $8,219.17 and a few odd mills. I now saw the necessity of being cautious and economical. Having recovered our breath, we began to look around for some means of reaching the treasure. We found a tree that had fallen against the the wall and were soon making our way up, slowly, for the branches were very thick and covered with thorny spikes. Our hands were lacerated, our faces scratched, arms and legs were pierced in a thousand places, but what of that—we were rich, no more work—no more worry—$8000 a day, at the lowest estimate, and if we chose to embark our capital in business we might double, treble, quadruple this amount— what were a few scratches to us—and it was no dream. We were there now, through the thick foliage, we caught plimpses of the glistening mass. It was real. Cautiously we worked our way out on a long branch and stepped on the ledge. There was a space about a foot wide where we could stand by leanfng against the cliff, we crept out there and spread our hands on the seam of bright yellow—clay, We did very little talking on our return trip. When we did indulge in conversation it was about something that happened ages ago. We seemed to take no interest in recent occurances.

One evening we came to a little cabin, if a roof supported by four poles might be so termed. It was miles from any path. The owner, his wife, three small children, a pig, two dogs and a half dozen chickens were comfortably settled for the night, but on our appearance, the good wife quickly drove out the pig and dogs, in order to make room for us. We stopped here over night and made glad the hearts of the whole family in the morning by distributing a hadful of *reals* among the children, though we felt we could hardly afford such extravagance after our recent experience.

Just as we were about to leave in the morning, I noticed some old books on a shelf close up under the roof. This was a great surprise and I begged the privilege of looking at them. Judge of my astonishment to find a copy of "Crowley's British Poets" a pocket edition of "Webster's Dictionary," printed in 1880, and a small testament. To have unearthed a diamond at this place would not have been more unexpected, we were at least ten leagues from any traveled road. Our squatter friend could not speak a word English, could not even read or write his own lanquge. How then had he become possessed of these literary treasures? On the fly leaf of the testament were the words, "From Mary, December 25th, 1883." That was all. Noting our curiosity, our host explained their presence, and the following is a synopsis of the story of the books. "One day in March, 1885, a traveller had appeared before the house, he was tired and hungry and begged "posado e cafe." Of course, he was invited to stay as long as he wished. He was not well. His mule, a large gray animal was turned loose to graze. The stranger had little appetite and soon sought his hammock. In the morning he was not able to get up. At noon he was delirious. At sundown— dead. Alone, unknown, with out a single article by which he could be identified. It was many leagues to the nearest town. There was but one thing to do, that was to bury him. This the squatter did as decently as circumstances would permit, his wife being his only assistant. There was nothing about his person that afforded the slightest clue as to his personality. In his pockets were found a few silver coins of the country and a small knife. He carried no arms; age about twenty-five, fair, full beard, light hair, blue eyes. In his saddle bags were found these books, a map of Honduras, nothing more. His blanket, hammock, books and coins await a claimant, all carefully preserved. The case was reported to the alcalde at the earliest opportunity, but no information was ever received. He was buried at the foot of a pine tree, just at the edge of the forest. Some stones were piled over the grave to mark the spot. That was all, and Mary, sister or sweetheart, who ever she may be, will know, if these words should meet her eye, that he, for whom she traced those faint lines, had every attention that rude, but kindhearted people could give. The supposition is that he was a young Englishman, who had become separated from his companions, but nothing certain is known."

We returned to the highway, feeling very poor indeed, but tried to bear our misfortune bravely and actually forgot all about it before we came in sight of the capitol.

It was 2 P. M. by the watch and the 20th of November by the calendar when our weary mules, with their dust covered riders, arrived at the crest of the pass overlooking the valley of the Rio Grand, from whence we caught our first glimpse of Tegucigalpa, with its white walls and red-brown roofs. The scene was very beautiful. The valley stretches away for miles, with here and there a shimmering line of silver, betraying the course of the river its banks fringed with stately ceiba trees or overhung by rocky precipices. Far beyond, the mountains rise like a vast cerulean wall, their summits lost in the clouds. The peculiar charm of the scene, however, to our eyes, wearied with the changeless green of the tropical forest, where we had been buried for months, was found in the wide stretches of cultivated lands, with here and there a 'dobe house surrounded by groves of orange or mango trees. Here we saw fields of corn, rice (the upland variety,) acres of beans and patches of vegetables, with an occasional space devoted to pineapples or bananas, and at rare intervals a clump of cocoanut palms; but the thought that filled the heart of the writer with joy, was deeper than the valley, higher than than the mountains, wider than the landscape, for he knew that one of those tiny white specks in the distance was a hotel, and once there the sad eyed mules would be turned out to graze in the meadows and the well-worn hammocks, pack saddles, high-topped boots and huge spurs would be piled together in a shed to rest indefinitely, and that he would enjoy the luxury of a bed and regular meals served on the table, with a chair for a seat and a printed bill of fare. Good bye tortillas, good bye frijoles; welcome soup, fish, roast beef, white bread, salads, and best of all pie—American pie!

If the reader thinks the writer over enthusiastic on this subject let him follow his example and loose himself in the depths of the wilderness of Yoro, with a hammock for a bed, a log for a table, a native for a cook, tortillas and frijoles for breakfast, frijoles and tortillas for dinner–and for supper–why, tortillas of course, with frijoles—tortillas baked on a stone, served on a board, sans salt, sans butter; but I almost forgot; we had coffee—black, powerful, all conquering, without milk or sugar; served in a gourd. All this was delightful for a week or two. The novelty of it was charming; it seemed like a dream at first, but it became terribly realistic as the months passed by. Swallowed up by the wilderness, lost to the world, no letters, no papers, no gossip, no familiar face, no familiar sound; but it is over at last. Before us lies the land of promise, the city of our desire—land of rest, of peace, of pie!

Tegucigalpa, the capitol city, is the largest town in Honduras, containing about 15,000 people, mostly natives, but having a fair sprinkling of American, English and German merchants, with a few French and a half dozen Chinese. The city is pleasantly situated on the banks of the Rio Grande, which is here spanned by the only bridge in the republic. This bridge is a notable structure, having been built about a century ago. The materials used are burned brick laid in a cement of peculiar hardness so that the whole seems as though hewn out of solid rock. The city has an elevation of 3,400 feet, and enjoys a delightful climate—a perpetual June with a mid-day temperature a little lower than Comayagua, while the nights are a little warmer. Like all old Spanish towns the houses are built of adobe, with wide projecting eaves that almost meet over some of the narrowest streets. Although the buildings are nearly all one story, I noticed one three story and several two story blocks on the principal business thoroughfare. All structures, both public and private, are built flush with the streets, which are paved from wall to wall with cobble stones, sloping down gradually from the sides to the center, an arragement that converts every street into a river during the rainy season.

CALLE REAL.—(ROYAL STREET) LIVINGSTON.

The town is practically fireproof. The massive walls, averaging four feet in thickness, are surmounted by roofs of burned tiles. There are no stoves, and no chimneys, the fire being built on the floor, the smoke escaping through the spaces between the rafters at the eaves, which are always left open for ventilation. Ordinarily they have no windows, all the light coming in through the large doorways, which gives the house somewhat the appearance of a cave; however, they are admirably adapted to the climate, being as cool as cellars in summer and almost as cheerful. There are a few wealthy families whose residences are palatial in extent and elegant in their appointments. These houses are built around an open court, with large doors and projecting windows facing both street and garden. In these, the drawing rooms and parlors are furnished in Oriental luxury. The windows are made a pleasing feature. Instead of sash and glass, they are fitted with iron screens wrought in fancy patterns, the designs often betraying great ingenuity and artistic ability of a high order. The floors are laid with costly tiles and covered with a profusion of rugs. Chairs, tables, stands, bookselves, etc., are made by the native workmen, who display great skill in carving the beautiful woods of the country, which seem especially adapted for the purpose by reason of their fine grain and rich, deep color. In the chambers one is astonished to find polished brass bedsteads hung with silk curtains, while doors and windows are richly draped with costly fabrics imported from Paris at an immense cost, for every case of goods must be carried by men or mules over eighty miles of mountain roads.

Tegucigalpa is an Indian word, or rather a combination of two Indian words, which, literally interpreted, means mountain of silver. It is the presence of this metal that gives the town what little prominence it enjoys aside from being the seat of governmant. Although there are no mines in the immediate vicinity, the city is the base of supply for a number of large concerns within four or five leagues, so, while there is no factory, or railroad, or carriages, or anything to suggest the activity common to a town of the same size in the United States, there is nevertheless considerable bustle on the streets. Long trains of mules are continually arriving and departing, with their noisy drivers clad in picturesque rags. Prospectors from other fields are coming in with high hopes, others are leaving the country, cursing their luck and hurling imprecations againt the republic and its representatives from the President down. Others, who have met with success, will tell you there is no other land equal to this. These cannot find language sufficiently glowing to express their admiration of the State and its institutions. Of course, as in all such cases, the truth lies between the two extremes.

I have only the friendliest feeling for these people. Wherever we went we were treated with the greatest courtesy, receiving every attention and assistance from all classes, beginning with the President and running down the scale to the humble citizen who represents the office of "Boots" at the "Americano," and who performed his duties with the air of a man who condescends to serve you, not that he cares for the insignificant *real* which you will drop in his hand, but because you needed his friendly aid.

But to return to the city. The only building worthy of mention, from an artistic standpoint, is the old cathedral, which is a really fine example of Moorish architecture, and when seen under the soft light of the moon becomes a dream of beauty. Scarred by revolutions, seamed by earthquakes, stained by the storms of a century, overgrown with grass and weeds, which have taken root in every crevice in roof and wall, this old structure with its picturesque towers and deep toned-bells, presents a most interesting study. The mint, a long, low building with walls so thick that hardly a sound of the heavy stamps is heard outside, would not attract attention except for the guard that patrols the square. From $15,000 to $25,000 per month represents its activity, I'm told. There is a beautiful little park filled with flowers and shrubbery, divided by walks laid out with geometric precision, with a rustic balcony hidden by flowering vines, from which the military band discourses music patriotic or pathetic, as the case may be. Here, too, is found a really fine equestrian statue of Francisco Morazan, the Washington of Honduras. This is the popular promenade, and if you wish to meet a friend, or enemy, all you have to do is to take a seat near the main entrance, and ten to one you'll find your man, or woman, for that matter, in less than a quarter of an hour, for here every one of any consequence will be found regularly taking their daily constitutional. Here comes a group of merchants walking as though for a wager and talking like machines, now a stately old don, sauntering slowly, never in a hurry, never surprised, but always polite, observing every requirement of etiquette with religious exactness, now a handsome senora of the old school, followed by a bevy of brighteyed senoritas, their pretty heads filled with frivolous fancies, absorbed from the latest French novels. Spanish ladies are all beautiful walkers, and, as an artist I feel privileged to admire these fairy-like figures floating by so airily, their delicate shoulders enveloped in clouds of lace that shimmer faintly, like a wreath of mist in the twilight. Here they come again their black eyes sparkling with mirth, cheeks aglow, ruby lips, teeth like pearls, glossy tresses arranged so carlessly, yet with what consumate art. Ah! beware young man! arrows are flying here and lucky indeed is the youth who escapes without a scratch.

If any of my readers should ever visit this city I am sure they will stop at the "Hotel Americano," not only because it is a pleasant place to tarry, but because it is the only hostelry in the city. This hotel enjoys some special favors under government protection and is the only public house I know of that receives regularly, a pension, if I may use the term, amounting to $40 a month by act of Congress. Here you will find almost everything you ever heard of and some things besides on the bill of fare. You will be sure of courteous treatment and cheerful attendants, but do not expect electric lights, or callbells, or telephone, and do not send for a cab or ask when the train will arrive; do not look for the hydrant, for all the water is carried from the river in huge jars, and you will get your share in due time; do not wait for the whistle at noon; do not listen for the screech of the locomotive or the discordant clang of its bell. The only sound of the night is the murmur of the water as it frets drowsily among the piers of the old bridge. Read, sleep, dream, and forget for a time all the worries, cares and restlessness of the great world abroad.

CHAPTER X.

TEGUCIGALPA—INTERVIEW WITH PRESIDENT BOGRAN—OFF FOR THE COAST—ARRIVE AT AMAPALA.

Tegucigalpa, however, is not always thus silent and restful; they have their feast days and national holidays, the former follow one another with frightful frequency. During these occasions there is rest for neither body nor soul. Pandemonium reigns. Noise—noise—noise—for centuries these people have racked their brains to invent instruments for producing sounds of the most unearthly character and infinite variety. So we have every device for the purpose that the mind can conceive, each fiendish contrivance run to its full capacity.

The fifteenth of September is a great national holiday and preparations for its celebration begins a week in advance of that date. Every night witnesses a preliminary outburst, each excelling the last, until the grand climax is reached on the evening of the day in question, which usually results in the loss of eyes, legs, arms, and heads sometimes.

Referring to my note book I find the following under date of September 11.—"Beautiful moonlight night: sitting on the upper gallery overlooking the court yard; busy scene; new arrivals constantly appearing covered with dust, strange costumes, miners attired in red flannel shirts, blue pants, huge riding boots, great jingling spurs, shaggy beards, some hopeful, others disconsolate; Mozos dashing hither and thither; a mixed crowd; clatter of dishes in the dining hall tells of appetites whetted by long rides over the mountains; from the bar comes the cheerful clinking of glasses and loud laughter, a confused murmur of many voices in many languages. Suddenly the church bells began to ring, all at once, not as we ring bells at home, but each one struck rapidly with a hammer, there are about twelve churches and each has from three to six bells. A man or boy is appointed to pound each one of these, striking hard and rapidly, horrible tumult: can the town be on fire? Impossible, there's nothing to burn, mud walls three feet thick, roofs tiled—fire-proof town. Suddenly a blaze of rockets lights the sky, next a flash of red light, followed by loud cheers, then white and blue lights follow, more yells, we go to the plaza, a dense crowd of men, women and children fill every available space, all laughing. talking, yelling, smoking. In the center of the square madly charging to the right and left was a bull, covered with a framework to which hundreds of roman candles were attached. These were connected by a slowly burning fuse. The effect was startling, the populous were fairly wild with excitement. Pushing our way through the struggling, screaming mass of humanity, we discovered that the "bull" was simply a skin skillfully stretched, with head and horns complete and was carried by two men, whose bodies were hidden within the framework, with the exception of their legs. The roman candles were sent in every direction into the crowd, rockets filled the sky, fire crackers and guns added to the carnival of noise, besides boys were beating tin pans, blowing tin horns, pounding woodens boxes. We wonder what invention will be brought into use to swell this din on the great 15th, and silently pray that we may be far away among the mountains." One day, longing for official society, I called an interpreter and together we made our way to the executive mansion by courtesy called the "palace," for the purpose of calling on the President.

The officer on guard bowed very low when I presented my card and invited us to be seated, while he handed the bit of paste board to a subordinate with orders to gfve it to the O. S., who in turn passed it to the I. S. and from him to a page, who carried it to the great man who presided over the destinies of the republic. In the course of a few minutes we were waited upon by an officer in brilliant uniform, who conducted us through some shadowy passages which finally led to a large, well-lighted and handsomely furnished apartment. Here we found the General surrounded by a number of officers of the army. He looked somewhat weary, but shook hands cordially. As he spoke only Spanish and French and the reporter nothing but United States and Cherokee, our conversation was not marked by any great degree of amination, however, with aid of the interpreter we got along pretty well. After a few preliminary remarks, the President inquired what "concession" I desired. When he learned that I was simply traveling for pleasure and was not seeking permission or assistance to drill wells or tunnels, build roads, construct canals or waterworks, and did not care to incorporate a company to manufacture ice or electric light, and would not dig gold, silver, iorn, copper, coal or salt, or even open a stone quarry or start a cracker bakery or a livery stable, in fact had no favors to ask, and no wish to engage in any business whatever, at the expense, and under the protection of the government, and furthermore hated work with as deadly a hatred as any Spaniard, he fell on my neck and wept. The scene was very affecting but as our time was now up, I disengaged myself from his warm embrace and with hearts too full for words, we silently shook hands and parted. Some persons may think this scene exaggerated and possibly it is, but it is impossible to exaggerate in regard to the "Snap Hunters," who are arriving every day with some great improvement scheme with which they would oppress this poor but happy people. Still they come, a never ending procession from France, Germany, England, the United States, schemers seeking "concesssions" from the government to secure the sole control of some wildcat operation, gigantic plans of development or improvement by which the republic is to reap millions and the projector, undying fame. Railroads, bridges, canals, highways, each have a loud representative at the Capitol filling the ears of the distracted Executive with their magnificient offers.

GEN. LOUIS BROGAN.

The day of our visit the President had been waited upon by an agriculturlist from Virginia, who has discovered that the hope of the republic lies in its agricultural resources, "all you need", he declared, is a few ideas in regard to the proper cultivation of the soil." He felt that his mission was to introduce these innovations and simply asked the privilege of cultivating a little patch ten miles square for a period of twenty years, the government to furnish the necessary labor and tools, which he vowed would be but a slight remuneration for the time and talent required to turn so much wilderness into a blooming garden.

There is a paper published here known as the "Honduras Progress." It is probably the only sheet in the republic printed entirely in English. It is not as large as the New York World (Sunday Edition,) consequently cannot give space to so many obselete jokes, though it does well for its size, four pages 10 x 14 inches; this territory is cleverly divided between advertising and anecdotes, with an occasional editorial when other matter cannot be found.

The Editor and proprietor, Dr. R. Fritzgartner, keeps fully abreast of the times, as times go in Honduras. The Doctor is also "Government Geologist," but this does not prevent his taking a hand in the weather which he tends to every week with the usual disregard to the wishes of the people; What makes it worse, he publishes the result regularly.

By consulting the columns of the Honduras Progress we find that for the seven days ending with March 21, 1892, the citizens of Tegucigalpa were forced to endure a "minimum" and "maximum" temperature as follows:

March 15,	64 F.	(Min.)	85 F.	(Max.)
" 16,	64	"	88	"
" 17,	65	"	86	"
" 18,	61	"	86	"
" 19,	63	"	83	"
" 20,	68	"	84	"
" 21,	68	"	87	"

That's a pretty fair lot of weather for one week, 453 minimum degrees to say nothing of 599 maximum degrees, the doctor ought certainly to be reprimanded for such reckless waste of material. That number of maximum and minimum degrees might have been spread over a whole month and the citizens would have been just as happy and well satisfied.

In connection with the weather department we find other information regarding the location of the Capitol City. We give it here so that if any reader should wish to find it he could do so with his eyes shut, almost. All that would be necessary would be to go to Greenwich, start west, but parallel with the line of the equator, walking, wading, swimming or flying, as the condition of the road might demand, to a point 87· 10 degrees, thence south, but parallel with some longitudinal line (you can take your choice) to another point 14· 15 degrees north of aforesaid equator. If, following the lines indicated, the traveler has kept resolutely on a level with the ocean, which of course would necessitate some tunnelling in places, he would find himself just 3,400 feet below the office of the enterprising H. P. Naturally he would take the elevator. All this is very interesting and instructive, and when the public comes to realize that every issue of the H. P. is loaded to the muzzle with information of equal value, the subscription list will swell rapidly.

THE CAMINO REAL NEAR PETOA.

The H. P. is a regular encyclopedia of useful knowledge, some of the facts are almost startling. For instance, under the head of "Merchandise imported in Honduras," we find under "Class A" a duty of 50 cents per lb. but notwithstanding this almost prohibitive tariff, there were imported during the fiscal year 20 lbs. sponges, 28 lbs. blue mass and 250 lbs. of guitar strings and 318 lbs. of garters. These facts are interesting, and the student of political economy may be able to figure out what became of those garters in a country where stockings are not in style. We never saw one, though the field for such goods seemed very large indeed. In Class X, the duty is 80 cents per lb. and the importations of riding gloves amounted to 5 lbs. while that of woolen shawls reached the alarming total of 2,905 lbs. Class XI with a duty of $1.50 per lb. tells a story of vanity seldom equalled by any other country. It includes billiard balls, jewelry, silks and velvet. Of the first 21 lbs. were entered, while the importations of silk shawls rose to 5,682 lbs! Don't tell us it costs nothing to dress in Honduras. This is the one indispensible article which the belles of Honduras demand, and which they will have regardless of consequences. They come in every imaginable shade and are brilliantly embroidered in colors equally striking, but when we remember that this one garment takes the place of hat, shoes, waist and skirt, and that the lady possessing one of these beautiful patterns with a pair of garters, is fully equipped for any emergency, we ought surely to look upon this expenditure as quite modest and commendable.

But the H. P. is still bubbling over with information, under another class we find the necessities of life, which includes absynthe, brandy, rum, etc., and we are not suprised to note the kind forethough of a considerate administration which has placed the tariff on these staples at 16 cents per lb. so that the 26 tons of brandy that the custom house records show to have been imported during the past year, only enriched the government to the amount of $8331.36 against $8523.00 received on account of silk shawls. Surely as long as the brandy tax can be kept below that of silks and garters there ought to be no cause for domestic strife.

There is other matter in the H. P. but we don't feel free to use it. The Editor permits us to say that the price of the paper is $2.00 per year strictly in advance. The "advance" clause is probably his little joke. But after all there is not a better, a worthier, or a kinder man in all Honduras, and the success that has been his has been fairly earned and well deserved, and his merit, as a gentlemen and scholar are freely acknowledged by his fellow citizens who unite in praising his work both as a Geologist and Journalist.

We left Tegucigalpa on the morning of the 14th starting about 4 p. m. We did this in order to escape the "racket" that had already begun. The distance to Amapala is about 75 miles, the road passably good with the exception of a few places where washouts had occured and a few other places where a half mile or so of track has been buried under an avalanche of rock and rubbish. The scenery was fine, but quite different from the Atlantic Coast. There was very little to suggest a tropical climate. The mountains were more rugged and barren, the trees, mostly oak and pine, with wide openings. We crossed some extensive fields of coarse gravel that would not support a blade of grass. The only vegetation found on these wastes was the cactus, which seem to delight in such surroundings.

As usual, we stopped when and where we chose. At one place we tarried to watch a "bull chase," this was on the 15th and the gallants had gathered at the little village of San Antonia to celebrate the event. All were dressed in their best and mounted on the tough little horses of the country. In the center of the plaza a huge bull was pawing the earth, bellowing fiercely. At a given signal the horseman approached, one of them being armed with a long, sharp pointed pike, with which he prodded his bullship until he charged, then away they flew. The game was to keep out of the animals way, while one or another would dash up behind the enraged beast, seize it by the tail, and by suddenly veering to the right or left, throw the animal. The one succeeding in this would be the winner, and all the rest would be expected to "treat." We saw the feat successfully performed several times and noted the growing hilarity of the crowd who were gradually being affected by the frequent doses of "Aguardiente." Once, the bull, quite discouraged, made a mad rush into a house and we heard loud sceams as the women and children fled out the rear door. As fast as one animal was worn out, another was procured, and thus the sport went on.

One morning we were startled by a mysterious sound, or rather a series of sounds that came apparently from the depths of the mountains—in all our lives we had never heard such dismal wails, sometimes they would sink to a dull groan, then gradually rise to a wild shriek, now a single voice, now a duet, now a chorus; as usual, when in doubt we appealed to Don Pedro, who at once set our minds at rest, though he seemed somewhat astonished if not actually annoyed by our ignorance. However, the worthy Don is nothing if not a diplomat, so he swallowed his idignation and smiling blandly informed us that there was nothing to fear, as the peculiar noise was produced by the very simple process of grinding cane in a native mill, and promised that we would pass the same before noon. The guide was right, about two hours later we saw a cloud of steam rising above the trees, just ahead of us, and were glad of an excuse for stopping a while; we found four scantily attired Indians in charge; they seemed socially inclined and we spent a pleasant half hour, looking over the plant, not that it required so much time, but simply because there was no hurry and Pizarro, in his companion seemed so well pleased with the scenery that we could not bear to interrupt their reveries.

Our friends were "boiling down" as our maple sugar makers would say, their object being to convert the syrup into sugar, which is of the coarsest quality, of a dark brown color, this is put up in small packages of one or two pounds, each of these being carefully wrapped in corn husks which were skillfully woven together at the ends so that when finished they somewhat resembled ears of corn. The outfit was not extensive, the machinery being of the most primitive pattern, the entire structure was made of timbers roughly hewn, the crushing apparatus was a marvel of complexity, consisting of a number of wooden rollers operated by a system of cogs and interlocking shafts, the whole being an invention of a native by the name of Julio Fiallos Ponciano Lozano, he he probably owned other names but they had escaped—however, his machine still stands a monument to his ingenuity. Although it had been in operation for more than quarter of a century it had never been oiled, and the frightful sounds produced by the creaking of the wooden mechinism can never be described—the motive power was found in a couple of small oxen—not more than half the juice was saved by the crude process, but that was a matter of small concern, as there was scarcely any market for the product, so the proprietor informed us. At one side a half dozen cattle were eagerly devouring the half crushed canes—we purchased a few packages at a *real* each—and left the proprietor and family feeling very proud and happy, for the words of praise and liberal patronage bestowed.

We arrived at San Lorenzo one afternoon about 2 o'clock. For several hours we had been traveling through a flat country almost barren. The heat was intense and it was with some pleasure that we discerned the huge iorn roofed sheds, of the Rosaria Mining Co. of New York, which were used as a general supply station for the mines operated by that corporation. At the time of our arrival the main structure was filled with giant powder, packed in cases and piled one on another from floor to roof.

While we rested in the grateful shade of these metal roofs, we could not help wondering where we would land in case the twenty tons of explosive should be found by a vagrant spark from the pipes of some natives who were lounging in the shadow of one of the walls, smoking quite unconcerned. A hundred yards away some other natives were cooking over a brush fire, which now and then started the dry grass in the vicinity and was only extinguished by a lively fight with wet blankets for weapons. However, no one seemed alarmed and we did not wish to appear to disadvantage, so we lit our cigars and lolled in the shade like the rest, nevertheless we wondered which one of the planets would receive us in case of an accident. Twenty tons of powder requires a good deal of room when it expands to its fullest capacity, and we knew it would be entirely too crowded for us on that coast, but we didn't mention it.

Here we parted with our mules—and were not sorry. From this point we would proceed by boat. Though we could not avoid a feeling of regret as we shook hands with our good angels for the last time, for they had proved very faithful, but angels as well as men must go their ways, so after an hours repose and a good square meal, father and son, each mounted on our riding animals and leading the two packs, started on the return trip, hoping to reach the village of Nacoame before nightfall.

It now occured to us to look for our boat, and presently we found it, a disreputable bungay, lying on one side in a mud bank, which bordered an oozy plain that stretched away to the westward and ended apparently in a wilderness of mangrove trees. Not a drop of water was in sight, yet we were to take the boat at this point, Meanwhile, the craft was straightened up by the united efforts of five wild looking creatures, who had been engaged to take us across to Amapala.

Amapala is the chief port of entree for the republic and its most important town on the Pacific coast. It is situated on Tigre Island in the Bay of Fonseca, seventeen miles from the mainland. Here we found Mr. Jacobi, special agent for the Rosario. He was on his way to New York, having been "buried twelve months" as he termed it "in Honduras." He was also bound for Amapala, so we embarked in the same vessel. It seemed very odd to be sitting here in the midst of a wilderness waiting for the ocean to come to us. To all appearances we might be a thousand miles from the sea, but there was our Bungay with its single square sail, and there were the villianous looking sailors stretched in the shade of the powder shed. They were a picturesque lot and wicked looking. Each wore a stout leather belt, which, in addition to supporting their linen pants served as a resting place for a massive, old time pistol dating back to the fifteenth century perhaps. They wore neither shoes nor shirt and for headgear a bright red handkerchief tied turban fashion answered every purpose. From beneath this lurid covering their long, black locks fell in straggling streamers. They looked like murderers. There were five of them thorougly armed. We were only three.

The wilderness of mangrove swamp extended in every direction for leagues. We were miles from any town, our valises were heavy with the silver coin of the country, night was approaching, the white herons were already returning from their distant feeding grounds, a lonely pelican was seen flying heavily, its great pouch distended with the fish it was carrying home to a hungry family. About 4 P. M. or a little later we saw the water swirling up through the forest to the west, another half hour it had crossed the flat marsh and washed the keel of our boat. It was a strange sight, a splendid sight, it advanced slowly but grandly. A long line of silver gleaming between the trees was the first evidence we had of its approach. On it came like a rapidly rising river, there was a pleasant murmur of tiny waves, the air became fresh, it was the air of the ocean, invigorating, life-giving, driving back the heavy malaria laden atmosphere of the swamps. In a little while our boat swung clear, passengers and crew took their places, the captain at the helm, while the four sailors seized the oars and soon were bearing down toward what seemed a solid wall of foliage, but just as we expected to be wedged fast among the maze of roots and decaying logs, the captain suddenly veered a point to the right and we glided into a narrow channel just wide enough to admit the boat. A couple of miles through a series of leafy tunnels brought to the open sea just at sunset. In a few minutes it was quite dark. The oarsmen pulled steadily. With each stroke they rose to their feet sinking back on the seat as the oars left the water, thus for four long hours they rose and fell with the regularity of machines. The sail was not used, the wind being unfavorable. The sea glowed with phosphorescent light, looking down in the clear water we could plainly trace the movements of the fish by this peculiar radiance.

We arrived at Amapala about midnight, finding all shops closed and streets deserted. Strolling along, what appeared to be the main thoroughfare, we were challenged by a sentry, who, when we failed to halt promptly, clapped his hands loudly and two other ragmuffins suddenly appeared. The two recruits were armed with rifles and seemed anxious to use them. They demanded an explanation. Mr. Jacobi, who speaks Spanish like a native, told them that we had come to take the town, but had changed our minds and were now simply looking for a hotel, and producing a bottle from his traveling bag he passed it to the guardian of the night who had first accosted us. He held it up a moment between his eyes and the sky, then throwing his head back placed the long, slim neck to his lips gradually increasing the angle of elevation until it stopped on the central bar of the southern cross. In the darkness, a stranger might have mistaken him for an astronomer, who had come out to study that splendid constellation, but we knew better. There was a low gurgling sound that was soothing to the ear. Although so dark, we could see a smile of satisfaction playing over the angular features, "gracias Senor, muches mas gracias," and added "Buena" as he passed the telescope to his companion, who elevated the instrument in the same way, although his interest seemed to be centered in a group of stars several degrees higher, and when the third fellow's turn arrived, we were not surprised to see him fix his gaze on the zenith where it rested until the last drop had been drained and those peculiar gurgling sounds quite ceased.

We were now on the best of terms. It's wonderful how a bottle of brandy smooths the way in this country. We had noted it's magic effect on former occasions. It's a regular Alladin's lamp, it breaks down every barrier, opens all the secret places. Our challengers now became our guides and leading us through a number of narrow deserted lanes, stopped before the only hostelry in the place, which was closed and dark, but not long. One of our friends turned his heavy gun into a battering ram and attacked the door with such vigor that the landlord soon appeared in a great rage, demanding "who in the d———l" we were and what we wanted at that time of night, but seeing the soldiers with their guns, he at once became very meek and inquired what he could do for us. Our friends then explained to him that we were a party of eminent Americans, who had just arrived on a tour of inspection and would stop with him several days. They said we were friends of Gen. Bogran and intimated that anything he could do for us would be appreciated by the President—so much for the molifing effect of a sip of brandy in the still hours of night. With this introduction, we were made welcome at once and the obsequeous inn-keeper hurried hither and thither in his efforts to provide for our comfort. Servants were rudely awakened and in less than thirty minutes the best the house afforded was brought forth. Less important guests were routed out and given cots or hammocks in the little court in the rear—anywhere at all to make room for the friends of the President. After a substantial lunch and a quite smoke, we sought our room, a large apartment containing three old fashioned beds protected by a canopy of netting, beneath which we plunged without loss of time. The house had become quite still, and the only sound of the night was the low moaning of the surf, beating hopelessly over the lava rocks that line the harbor.

DR. FRITZGARTNER.

Amapala is a small place very similar to other Spanish towns, except that the buildings are frame, many of them of a most temporary character; population about 3,000.

In my note book I find the following entrees :

September 20—Met a genuine Carib in the park today, recognized him at once as a Belize man, not that I had ever seen him before but by his voice and expression, it belongs to Belize alone and once heard will never be forgotten. I asked him what he was doing so far from home. He said, ' I'm a prisoner sah!"—a prisoner! I felt a sudden chill, had I wandered unconsciously into forbidden ground? perhaps I was a prisoner also. Here was this man apparently free as the air, stretched at full lenghth in the shadow of a large tree, smoking most comfortably. Further inquiry developed the fact that he had been detected smuggling sugar into Truxillo and had been brought over here to work three months on the public improvements. A little distance away I discovered a couple of soldiers, his guards, both were sitting in the shade, smoking and chatting. Occasionally during the day the prisoner was called upon to move some boards or carry some mortar for a mason, who was engaged in building the foundation or pedestal for a monument. As the mason rested nearly all the time his attendant was left to sit and dream or wander about the place at will. He seemed quite contented and would have been better pleased with a years sentence.

September 21—Still waiting for the steamer, getting impatient —later, have made arrangements to cross the bay in a Bungay, start to-night about 11 P. M. anticipate a disagreeable trip, the captian says he can make the distance, about 90 miles in 20 hours.

September 22—Board Bungay, Bay of Fonseca, left port 11 o'clock last night, very hot, wind dead against us, packed in like sardines, frequent showers, sail useless, men rowing, town still in sight.

Evening—Still on board, tired, 14 passengers beside the crew, every inch of space filled, only change of position is from sitting to standing, Chinaman deathly sick, lays in the bottom of the boat like a log and groans, here we meet the long, rolling swell of the Pacific, nearly every wave washes over the side of the Bungay, two men are forced to desert the oars and bail, heat excessive—a large whale, a few hundred yards to the leeward, pursued by sword fish, lashes the sea into a white froth. The huge creature leaps out of the water, falling back with a tremendous splash, exciting scene—will he cross our path? We are loaded almost to the water's edge, if we should be struck we would certainly be lost; never was combat watched greater interest, and never were men more relieved when we saw them drifting to the northward, where we could see the white foam glistening in the sunlight for nearly an hour longer.

September 23—Still on this horrid Bungay, nearly dead from hunger, thirst and loss of sleep, provisions mostly ruined by salt water, only a few crackers remain and those well soaked, but we are across and sailing up the Rio Grande, where we will land some time to-day. Later—We landed about 10 A. M. at the custom house, the most desolate place I have ever seen, high tide covers all the land for miles around and this miserable hut stands on stilts about eight above the ground. No other habitation in sight, nothing but mangrove swamps, stretching away forever.

Tampesqua, September 24—We thought morning would never come, the air was filled with mosquitoes and we at their mercy, no sleep, spent the night in battle and got the worst of it, sorry looking crowd, fairly raw from thousands of bites, faces red and swollen. This was our introduction into Nicaragua. Carts arrived about 10 A. M., never so glad to see anyone before, the driver lost no time, blindfolded the team—only way to keep them still, being distracted by flies. Started at a 11 A. M. through a dreary forest, heavy two-wheeled carts, wheels solid wood, the creaking could be heard for miles. Away we go, over logs, stones, bump—bump—bump—will we live to reach town?

Chinandega, 25—Town of about 10,000 built on a level plain, the long, muddy, unpaved streets stretch away into the distance lined with houses of every form and color, some adobe, but more frame and many bamboo, with thatched roofs, through whose basket-like walls the movements of the inmates are easily observed. Line fences represented by cactus hedges. Behind these living walls we we sometimes caught glimpses of shady little yards with orange trees, or a few stalks of bananas. A 5 o'clock gun arouses the people in the morning and from that hour tell 10 A. M. the streets present a busy appearance."

We now felt that our troubles were over. It seemed to us that we had advanced a thousand miles during the past twenty-four hours. Here we were, enjoying our ease with all the comforts of a good hotel, the "Reforma," this time yesterday we were suffering unspeakable torture in the horrible swamps of Tampeaqua. Here we would take the train, and from this on we would travel by rail or steamer.

Nicaragua boasts but one railroad, but it is well cared for and trains run regularly making good time. The road is kept in excellent order. The government looks after it, and having nothing for her vagabond soldiers to do, they are employed to care of the road and stations. The track is well ballasted, all grass and weeds kept closely cut for a distance of 25 feet on each side of the rails. Station houses are of modern design and neatly painted. Officers polite and attentive. Passengers are divided into three classes. First, second and third. The highest rate, which pays for a seat in a modern coach, is 5 cents per mile. A second class ticket entitles the holder to the same privileges excepting, that the seats run lengthwise of the car and the traveler must sit with his back to the window—in other respects the coach is just as desirable and the majorty of tickets sold, read "Second Class," the rate being 3½ cents. Third class tickets are sold at the low rate of 2 cents per mile and the purchasers are carried in cattle cars, provided with rough board seats.

There is no danger of having to stand during a journey by rail, in Nicaragua, as the company will only sell as many tickets as there are seats, so after securing a ticket there is no occasion to make a wild rush for the train, as your place will be reserved. A half dozen soldiers each armed with Sprinfield repeating rifles and under the command of a flashily uniformed officer, will be found at every depot, guarding alike the interests of the road and its patrons.

Trains are usually filled, and the road seemed to be in a prosperous condition. The engineers were all Americans as well as the General Manager.

We left Chinandega about 8 o'clock, September 26, and two hours later found ourselves in the metropolis of Nicaragua, the ancient city of Leon.

HOMEWARD BOUND.

CHAPTER XI.

CITY OF LEON—AN HONEST CABMAN—MOMOTOMBO—STORM ON LAKE MANAGUA—ARRIVE AT THE CAPITOL,—ITS INDUSRRIES.

The city of Leon contains about 30,000 inhabitants and covers an area sufficiently extensive to accommodate 3,CC0,CC0 or thereabout. Here we found many cabs awaiting the arrival of the train, not to mention the donkey carts and ox teams. A scene so full of life and hustle was inspiring. There were news boys, bootblacks, porters and many women carrying large wooden trays piled high with confectionery, sweet bread, pies, fruits of the country. Competition was brisk among the various venders, and our party was soon surrounded by a boisterous crowd, who tried to force their wares on our attention. Finding ourselves unable to patronize each of these vociferous applicants, we made a dash for a cab bearing the legend "Hotel Leon de ora," and a few moments later we found ourselves before this picturesque hostelry. The "Leon de ora" is not the largest or finest hotel in the world, but to us, fresh from the wilds of Honduras, it seemed a palace—a paradise. Here we enjoyed all the luxuries of civilization. Thanks to American enterprise, the railroad that connects this city with Managua brings a plentiful supply of ice every morning from the plant at the capitol. This means a great deal to the dweller in tropical countries. Cards tacked up about the house announced, "ice water 5 cents a glass, unless served with other drinks at the bar, in which case it is free."

During our stay at the "Leon de ora," we never saw a glass of water sold, but the bar tender was kept busy giving it away as a premium to purchasers of cocktails at 20 cents each or plain brandy at 15 cents. There is a good deal of history lying around Leon, and the neighboring towns, but it is too familiar to bear repeating. There are the usual number of old churches with crumbling walls over grown with grass and moss, tile roofs, with eaves projecting far over the street, hundreds of small shops, a few large stores, the average amount of bell ringing, rattling of kettle drums, blowing of horns.

A large number of antique vehicles, drawn by hungry looking horses, patroled the streets waiting for passengers, who seldom appeared. We thought it would be a philanthropic act to hire one of these turnouts and thus assist some poor but honest citizen. We accordingly hailed the sorriest looking individual we could find. He came quickly, his face beaming with delight. We were the first customers he had struck in three long, tropical days, so he said. As he stuck to his native tongue and we stood closely by our own, there is a possibility of errors creeping into this report, however, he seemed very glad to secure our trade, and made us understand quite clearly that he would charge only one little degraded silver dollar for a whole hours service and that during that brief space of time he would drive further than any other man in the city. We soon learned that Leon held at least one honest cabmen, too honest by far. In less than five minutes we were trying to explain that we had made a mistake, we did not want to ride, he was quite welcome to the dollar, it was only a silver dollar and not worth much, only let us out—but he would not hear to it—he understood that the dollar was a debased and worthless coin, but we had given it to him in good faith and he was glad to get it, and he must give us full value for the same. During this argument we were flying along at full speed, every few yards our relentless Jehu would give a wild whoop and cut the horses with a long but elastic switch, which acted as a mild stimulant. We were now rushing through long, muddy streets lined with thatched huts surrounded with cactus hedges. Wild, unkempt women stared after us in utter bewilderment, naked children fell over each other in their efforts to escape destruction, five hundred dogs followed in our wake, (the number is estimated, there may have been more) they were large, small and medium and the chorus, ranging all the way from the low bass of a lean and hungry hound, up to the lofty soprano of an English terrier—produced a musical medley seldom equaled—certainly never excelled. Thus we tore along at full gallop, up one narrow lane, down another. These back streets were unpaved and deep chuck holes filled with water occured at frequent intervals. Every time we plunged in to one of these dark abysses, there would be a cloud of muddy spray thrown over everything in the vicinity. We tried in vain to explain that we were in no hurry, begging our driver to take his time—two hours, three hours, a half a day, a day if necessary, we would cheerfully pay him at regular rates. Money was no object to us, none whatever, but he was not to be moved. The more we argued, the louder he yelled and the harder he plied his lash. Now we struck the main thoroughfares. These were paved with cobble stone and bordered by shops of every description. We thought certainly he would now reduce the speed; but we were disappointed; on the contrary he increased his efforts. We passed like a metor; the stores with all their array of parti-colored goods seemed like flying ribbons on either hand, no individuality, no detail, like a picture of new school, broad bands of color nothing more. We passed dozens of ruined churches, the great cathedral of St. Peter, the plaza, the depot, only one third of our time used up. We were nearly dead with the jolting. Could we survive forty minutes longer? It seemed impossible. We tried to induce him to get down and take a drink, but he was a temperance advocate and could not be moved. On—on—we were leaving the city now, over a soft dirt road. What could have struck the man, was he crazy; not at all, we were going to see the "Pantheon," everybody wanted to see that, he said. It was two miles out, the road was fairly good, we were thankful that the authorities had selected this remote site for a burrying ground. We actually enjoyed the ten minutes it took to reach the place of monuments. The country was beautiful, recent rains had revived vegetation, the fields were well tilled, hedges neatly trimmed, the grass of that tender green that marks the new growth, many flowering shrubs lined the way, while the monotomy of the remote forest was broken by masses of gorgeous color, caused by the blossoming of wild fruit trees. White, pink, purple and deep crimson added a charm to the landscape. Beyond the forest the foot hills rose, and even at this distance we could discern the pale green tints of the rice fields, and dark squares that represented the coffee plantations. Still farther away the Marabios range of mountains, filled the horizon, culminating in the volcano of Momotomba, whose barren summit is clearly visible from here—"Le Pantheon!" as our guide announced the name of the cemetery, he brought his prespiring team to a stand, and we were allowed to dismount for the first time—we thanked our tormentor for this brief respite, even offering him an extra dollar—which to our great joy he indignantly refused to accept. We are among the tombs, a fair sort of grave-

yard, all new, white and glaring, the trees and shrubs have just
been planted, workmen are still employed laying out and constructing the walks. Some day this will be a beautiful place, when the
dazzling marble takes on the warm gray tones of age, mottled with
dark brown patches and the ivy climbs to the top of the tall shaft,
when the richly carved tombs are covered with silvery moss—then
this place will be interesting. By that time the authorities will
have become lax and the untrimmed trees will mingle their
branches across these barren paths, there will be deep shadows
with patches of sunlight falling between, the song birds will find
it a quiet place to rear their broods, the beautiful and harmless cha-
meleons will dart here and there reflecting all the colors of the
rainbow, bees will hum among the flowers and butterflies play
hide-and-seek in the fragrant groves. Lovers will wander here
and poets and all the good for nothing tribe, which the busy world

ROUGH RIDING.

dispise, but which the busy world would be loath to lose nevertheless. We had used up ten minutes on the way out to this desolate
place and spent ten more grumbling over it and were now ready to
return. Twenty minutes yet, would our hour never end? If it
was not that we were two miles from the "Leon de ora," we would
abandon the craft and let it drift back at its own gait, but we are
too lazy for the walk this hot day. We take our places, the driver
mounts the box the long slender rod whistles through the air, the
horses leap forward in anticipation of the blow—ten minutes and
we strike the cobbled streets again, we beg to be let off, but no, we
have paid for an hour and we must have the worth of our money.
He would not have it said that he had cheated a stranger out of
full ten minutes, so we race through street after street, up hill and
down, scattering the crowds as we go and followed by a procession
of mongrel curs. That last ten minutes seemed like an age, but

just as we were about to make a desperate leap for "liberty or death," the coach came to a sudden stand and we found ourselves in front of the hotel, our hour was up; this exciting experience was followed in the evening by a grand "Feista" in honor of the Virgin Mary with the usual din of bells, bands, cannon and fire works. After dinner we took a stroll through the plaza in front of the famous cathedral of St. Peter. It looked very beautiful indeed at a little distance, its lofty walls bathed in the ruddy light of the setting sun.

This huge building was begun in 1706, but so great was the undertaking that it was not completed until 1743. During the thirty seven years employed in its construction, over $5,000,000 were expended. At the time of our visit, it was undergoing repairs and an army of workmen were engaged in redressing the walls, cleaning and regilding the splendid alters. Wax figures of the Virgin, the infant Saviour, the Crucified Lord, and a number of celebrated prelates adorned the walls. There were also some very fine paintings imported from Paris. A narrow, winding stair of stone, leads to the tower, where we found a modern clock and the huge bells that may be heard for leagues around. The roof is of solid masonry, covered with cement that seems quite indestructable. The vastness of the structure astonishes one. A regiment of soldiers might camp here and be in no wise crowded. We wandered over this quiet plain of stone for a full hour, loosing ourselves among the wilderness of towers, observatories and secret passages. From this point of vantage we had a splendid view of the city which lay at our feet like a map. The various public squares looked like green patches in a huge quilt, while the solidly built portions were represented by blocks of red with yellow lines between, where we could see the people passing to and fro like ants. Beyond the outskirts of the town was a rim of cultivated fields, growing dim in the twilight, still further the mountains rose vague and indistinct like a bank of clouds. So pleasant the breeze, so fascinating the scene, we lingered until the stars began to peep forth and hundreds of Roman candles and thousands of rockets sprang upward as though to greet the heavenly host that looked down so serenely on all this confusion of light and sound. At the time of our visit, travel had been greatly stimulated by the reports so diligently circulated to the effect that work would be commenced at once on the "Canal"—that tremendous joke of the Hon. Warner Miller—consequently hundreds of persons were attracted to Nicaragua, and the hotels were crowded with despondent victims, many of whom had recklessly invested their entire capital in the effort to reach this Eldorado, only to find a country full of idle men, in which the annual revolutions had paralyzed every industry, and business of all kinds was at a stand—conditions which are considered normal by the lazy, thriftless natives, who seem perfectly content to lie at full length in the shade of the crumbling walls during the day and wander around the city at night, playing and singing as free from care as the buzzards that line the roadways, apparently. But Americans cannot exist in this happy-go-lucky style, they must live at the hotel, and the landlord must be paid. Three of these nomads arrived the evening of the Fiesta. They had traveled overland from Tegucigalpa, Honduras, where the closing of the Rosaria mines had thrown a large number of men out of employment. The glowing accounts published by the literary staff of the Canal Co., had reached the remote mining camps of the neighboring state and the disappointed gold seekers now turned toward Greytown in crowds.

Greytown is the eastern terminous and the point from which the work is supposed to be directed. Careful inquiry revealed the fact that no one in Nicaragua took the matter seriously, no interest was manifested in the enterprise, no faith placed in the promises of the company. But the scheme had been systematically and successfully boomed in the States, and stock to the amount of $80,000,000 had been subscribed, of which we are told about 6½ per cent. had been paid in and absorbed—by whom? Experts declare that all the improvements of any permanent value that have been made since the present company began operations, have not cost more than $100,000 or about 20 per cent. of the amount collected. So declares Mordecia Endicot, Naval Engineer, who was one of the government commission appointed to look over the property with a view of discovering, if possible, the actual conditions existing; whether the report of this commission is true or not, we do not pretend to say, but whether true or false, the logician finds himself driven irrisistly to one of two conclusions, either of which the promoters would not care to accept—at least publicly —viz: that a very small proportion of the $5,200,000 collected has been used—or, if this amount has been paid out for the improvements represented the total cost of the enterprise will run into hundreds of millions, and the time required will be reckoned by decades rather than years.

From Leon we proceeded to Managua, the capitol city, the distance was not great, but it included a trip across the lake from which the city takes its name. The scenery along the road was charming. We passed a number of populous towns. As soon as the train stopped at the station we would be surrounded by a crowd of men, women and children crying out their wares, all of native manufacture, fruits, flowers and curios, such as cocoanut shells, stained jet black, polished and engraved in intricate designs, showing a degree of skill quite surprising, considering the rude tools with which the natives perform the work. We were approaching the great volcano of Momotombo, its towering crest rose higher and higher and when we arrived at the village of La Paz about 10 A. M., we found ourselves at its very base; its grand outline filled the whole eastern horizion; it was a beautiful and impressive sight. The following sketch is clipped from the Indianapolis Journal:

"The village of La Paz, Nicaragua, situated on the shore of Lake Managua, is a place of small importance. "Our principal businesss here was to look at the mountain whose summit has never been trod by human feet. When the writer sailed from New Orleans three years ago he determined to make a special study of volcanoes, not from a scientific standpoint, but in an artistic sense, for they are not devoid of picturesque features, especially those situated within the tropics. Momotombo is a giant, standing 7,200 feet in his stockings; he is "rockribbed and ancient," and seemed to me to combine every quality a first class volcano should possess. He is bald-headed and smokes incessantly after the manner of his tribe. He stands beside the lake and waves his white plume a mile and a half above the waters that ripple at his feet.

Momotombo is the highest of the Marabios Range, and is one of the greatest purely volcanic masses in existence. True, the summit of Cotopaxi is over 18,000 feet high, but the base, properly speaking, begins at an elevation of nearly 14,000 feet above the Pacific. Here we have the whole grand pile in view at one glance, the shore-line marking the beginning of the ascent, which is barely 200 feet above the sea. The first 2,000 feet which rises gradually for three miles is covered with a dense tropical forest, dark, dank and dismal, the haunt of serpents, scorpions and myriads of stinging insects. The trees are covered with vines and creepers and support an endless variety of orchids. In this lower belt droves of monkeys find a congenial home; above this is a second belt of woodland, but more open, with wide spaces of barren rock and grassy glades. The trees here are mostly oak and pine, and the acorns furnish food for the wild hogs which claim this region by right of conquest, but who hold their title only by superiority of numbers and eternal vigilance, and even then fall frequent victims to the fierce appetite of the mountain lions whose epicurean tastes are particularly gratified by the flavor of a young porker. At four thousand feet all traces of vegetation disappear, and the vast cone rises abruptly, an unbroken mass of lava and scoria, to the yawning crater, whose mysterious depths have never been explored.

Long years ago some pious monks thought to cover themselves with glory and add lustre to the records of the holy church by planting a cross on the highest point. The fiery old monarch smiled grimly as he watched these pretentious beings creeping upward, slowly, laboriously. Now cutting their way step by step, through the all but impenetrable jungle, now scaling huge walls of basaltic rock that he had reared in infant sport ages past. On they came, slowly, painfully, but bravely withal, burning with religious zeal, dragging the ponderous emblem. They had passed the forest zone, the last stunted pine was now far below; around and ahead stretched a world of cinders and volcanic debris. Here and there masses of black, igneous rock and blocks of pumice stone broke the otherwise smooth outline of this mighty ash heap. Undismayed by the awful desolation, they boldly entered this treacherous field of shifting ashes. Twenty-five miles away the blue line of the ocean was distinctly visible; below them, spread out like a map, with every detail accurately penciled, lay the lake and river, with a dozen villages half hidden among orange groves; far to the northwest the white walls of the Cathedral of Leon gleamed faintly through the blue haze. The angle of ascent was now increased to forty-five degrees, and the men sank to their knees in the yielding surface, raising clouds of blinding dust.

From the interior of the mountain came a low, premonitory rumbling, like the bellow of an angry beast, low, deep and fearful.

It was Momotombo's warning to these human insects; it was as if he said, "Thus far shalt thou come, but no further." But the voice was unheeded. With a muttered prayer they pressed on, defying the giant, who from his smoky throne had witnessed the rise and fall of continents a thousand years before the dawn of history, perhaps. Ah! To be challenged by these midgets,! Momotombo shook with wrath, and, lo, the desecrators of his solitude were no more.

Just what caused the catastrophe can never be known, but the supposition is that in their struggle to advance they started a slide which soon became an avalanche, sweeping down with resistless force, burying the pious adventurers a hundred feet deep—not one escaped, and later explorers have been unable to find any trace of the ill-fated party.

Some idea of the difficulties to be encountered in making the ascent may be formed when it is stated that the last stretch, of 3,000 ft. is almost as steep as a church roof, being traversed in many places by deep fissures, from which clouds of steam and deadly gases rise continually, so that the traveler is in constant danger of being suffocated should he escape the slides which are almost sure to occur, the whole upper portion of the cone being composed of loose dust and detached rocks which the slightest disturbance will bring down in a destructive avalanche. And so it happens the crater has never been visited by man.

Great characters love to associate with their equals. Momotombo is no exception; therefore he occasionally invites a thunder storm to spend an evening in social chat. At first their voices are heard murmuring indistinctly, as they discuss some choice bit of gossip, but as the hours roll on the mirth increases, fed by the red hot cheer of the sulphurous larders, until the earth trembles with fear of the mad riot. In the morning, however, all signs of tumult have disappeared. There he stands smoking tranquilly, extending the hand of peace to all the elements of earth and air. Age has now cooled the passions of youth, and though he frowns darkly at times, his anger is short-lived and easily appeased; a puff of blacker smoke or a spurt of ashes relieves the pressure, and he resumes the calm indifference that has characterized him for more than a century. Not so his diminutive neighbors, who indulge in so much fuss and fume, that unawary observers are often misled by their clatter. Especially is this true of Conseguiana, who, though boasting an altitude of only 3,800 feet, is a regular little "spitfire" and throws out such volumes of smoke and dust in her jealous fits as to effectually hide her great rival. Her last outburst occured in 1835 when she sought to establish her superiority beyond cavil, by speading a coat of ashes ten feet thick over a vast tract of Nicaragua's best grazing lands; the area thus destroyed is roughly estimated at 300 square miles. On this occasion the finer dust was carried a distance of 400 leagues. At Kingstown, Jamaica, 700 miles away, the air was darkened by the cloud and streets and houses covered by the fine particles. Merchants exper-

ON LAKE MANAGUA.

ienced much annoyance and loss from the effects of the shower which, impalpable as air, penetrated the closest fiting cases, watchmakers and jewelers being especially unfortunate.

We tarried many days at a little cafe, in front of which, in the cool shade of a pair of mango trees, we lay in our hammocks, smoking the delicate and fragment cigarettes our landlord's pretty daughter Bonita rolled for our especial benefit. If at times we fell into a doze, I'm sure we were to be excused, in a land where the atmosphere is even heavier than that of the famed "Sleepy Hollow," where the dear old Knickerbockers slumbered on from generation to generation, until finally swallowed up by the advancing tide of modern enterprise; but mostly our eyes were turned towards the mountain, dreamily watching the shadows of the clouds as they glided slowly across it. The low murmur of tiny waves on the pebbly shore, the hum of insects among the blossoms overhead, the distant thrumming of a guitar, combined with the drowsy atmosphere, filling our hearts with a sense of restful peace. Every day was a poem, every night a delightful interlude. Why not remain in this peaceful seclusion? Let those whose minds are tormented with vain ambition continue the mad struggle for wealth or fame, or place—glittering baubles that reward for a moment a life of toil; hardly have they been secured when the hand that grasps them shrivels in death, and the tinsel toys become a source of contention among quarreling successors.

The sun had set, and the mantle of night was drawn over the lower world, but the high crest of the mountain held the rosy light of evening, the upper fields of broken lava and scoria glowed with life and warmth, the deep gorges that scarred the vast dome were traced in dark blue lines on a ground of pale violet that gradually melted into a brilliant orange at the summit, the whole standing out in bold relief against a sombre sky. From the depths of the crater a luminous cloud rose slowly to a height of a thousand feet, where it spread out in all directions, a canopy of gold. This was our hero's hour of triumph. He had no rivals now, the tallest of his envious neighbors was lost in the gathering shadows, he alone remained visible, grand, glorious, invincible."

We boarded the little steamer which lay waiting at the end of a long pier, which has been built out in the lake. We found the captain, paid our fare, ($1.50) and settled down to enjoy the four hours sail across this usually serene bit of water.

The day was beautiful, not a cloud was to be seen, the air clear as crystal, the sky a deep, steely blue. We steamed slowly along the base of the volcano, watching the white vapor rising from the crater and drifting away to the southward. The shore line was picturesque, consisting of bright green glades, broken here and there by rocky precipices, overhung with vines. The boat was crowded with natives, who were returning to the capitol from a sort of a religious pilgrimage to Leon, where they had taken part in the festivities of the previous day.

They were mostly women and they lay around on the bales of goods in graceful attitudes, a few were reading French novels, but the larger number put in the time smoking and sleeping by turns. About three o'clock we noticed a sudden commotion among the boat hands. The captain hurried here and there shouting orders in Spanish, men flew to the hold and returned with great rolls of canvass which they spread over the goods that were piled compactly on the deck. Then they lashed every loose thing fast, weaving a net work of heavy cables across the canvass, covering and tying down securely to the rail; meanwhile the crowd of natives began to weep and pray. We looked around for some sign of storm but could see none. The sun was shining brightly, the water rippled about the bows in bright green eddies, we could not understand all this haste. Far away to the south a dim vapor was visible, not dense enough to be called a cloud, simply a hazy appearance, but the sailors knew what it meant and so did the natives. It was the sure sign of the dreaded "Chubasco," or tornado. This film of haze rapidly thickened until in less than ten minutes the southern horizon dissappeared and a heavy black curtain rose in its place. On it came rising rapidly, extending to the right and left, blotting out hill, plain and mountain heights. Now we could hear the roaring of the wind as the left wing mowed a wide swath along shore, then we watched its advance across the lake, a long white line of torn water marked its passage. Clouds of spray rose like steam, the sun was eclipsed by the dense vapor —we were enveloped in darkness—the storm was upon us. It seemed impossible for our little boat to survive in such a sea, or that such a small body of water should produce such tremendous waves. The steamer rolled like a log but the pilot kept her head to the wind. For two minutes, which seemed like hours, the midnight blackness continued, and the noise of the tempest cannot be described. The water poured over the hurricane deck and found its way under the door of the captain's cabin, whither as many as could squeeze in, had taken refuge. Furniture, chairs, men, women, books, papers, stationery, pens, ink, cuspidors, hats, baskets, fruits, cakes and candy were churned up together, many of the women to ill to stand fell on the floor, where they shrieked or prayed by turns. The men endeavored to keep an upright position by clinging to the slender beams overhead. Some of them swore, others laughed, while a few joined the women in frantic supplications to "San Antonia." This was our first experience with a "chubasco" and we were quite satisfied. It was soon over. Half an hour later the sun was shining brightly, but the waves still rolled uncomfortably. Twelve miles away we could discern the city of Managua, simply a long line of white and pink spots on a pale blue ground of low hills. As we came nearer, our glasses were brought to bear on the distant port, hundreds of people crowded the wharf. When we arrived about 5 P. M. we began to realize the force of the storm, a wooden town would have been swept into the lake, as it was, many houses were damaged, roofs blown away, trees uprooted and the streets filled with debris. The crowd was now accounted for. They were the friends and relatives

Carriage of State — Chinindega Nicaragua

of the passengers who had come to welcome them as returned from the grave. There was so much embracing and weeping that we felt lonely.

After looking about for a suitable object to cry over, we found a sorry looking cabmen and fell—not in his arms—but in his coach. He drove us to the "Hotel Central," kept by Mr. Haslam, an Englishman.

Managua, besides being the capitol city, is the most enterprising town in the state, having a population of about 12,000 with quite a number of factories. The scene along the lake front presented an animated appearance. Jets of steam rising here and there among the trees indicate the presence of mills of various kinds, the buzzing of saws and hum of machinery made pleasant music. The sandy beach for more than half a mile was in possession of the women, whose lives are devoted to the destruction of clothing.

These groups of scantily attired women, with their black hair streaming in the wind, surrounded by piles of gaudy colored goods, delight the eye of the character sketcher, who finds here an inexhaustable mine to draw from. As fast as the pieces are washed they are stretched on the ground to dry, being anchored by a row of stones around the edge. To the children life seems one long holiday—they congregate here to race on the sand or swim in the surf, where they ride the waves like birds, or kick up their heels and dive into the g.een depths, only to re-appear forty feet away, their black heads shining like polished ebony.

Conspicuous among the enterprises of the city is the plant for the manufacture of artificial ice. The buildings of the company face the lake and being of modern design, present a fine appearance. The machinery, which includes all the latest improvemets, was supplied by the Consolidated Ice Machine Co., Chicago, Ill., and the inventors deserve the thanks of all who live in tropical countries. This plant was running to its full capacity, supplying all the towns and cities touched by the railroad. The manager was an American, of course.

Near the ice factory we found a large machine shop and foundry, known as the "School of Arts." It was built and maintained by the government, we were informed, as a training school for natives, who were placed there under competent instructors in order that they might gain a thorough knowledge, not only of machinery, but pattern making, moulding, wood working and finishing. However, the natives did not take kindly to such menial labor and very few graduates resulted. At the time of our visit, the "school" had degenerated into a repair shop for the railroad, and as such, gave employment to a couple of dozen men. As usual we found the Superintendent a native of the United States. He complained bitterly of having to train the ignorant natives, who show no inclination to acquire a mechanical education. Most of his assistants, he informed us, were the sons of wealthly parents, who had placed them there in order that they might be kept busy during the period that is supposed to be devoted to the sowing of wild oats. They took no interest in the work and never lost an opportunity to slip away and have a "time," all of which had to be overlooked, owing to the high social standing of their families.

The new Palace, as these little republics insist on calling the buildings of the executive department, faces the principal plaza near the center of the town. It is a fine structure, as far as completed, when finished it will occupy the entire square. The plaza itself is being improved, by the planting of trees and shrubbery.

An attractive feature of the city is its public library, containing about 10,000 volumes, a large reading room provided with comfortable chairs. Here we found all the great national newspapers, magazines, etc. The walls were hung with the portraits of those unfortunate patriots, who had been selected by an ungrateful people to serve in fear and trembling, for a term of four years, providing they were not found out by the bullet of an assassin or disposed of by some jealous rival, for in these countries revolutions rise with suddenness of the "chubasco," sweeping across the land leaving a trail of blood and charred ruins. The political sky may be perfectly serene in the morning, and night find the republic at the mercy of a hungry horde of rebels who respect no law, human or divine.

During these periodical outbursts, murder and rapine mark the passage of either army; women and children fall victims to the blind rage of zealots, equally ignorant, equally enthusiastic, whether they belong to the forces of the government or the rebels —only echoes of these conflicts reach the outside world, the meager dispatches that form but a drop in the ocean of news published daily by the metropolitan press, convey no idea of the horrors that are being enacted. While here we spent a pleasant evening with Mr. Willis, U. S. Consul, and incidently learned something of the minor trials of those self-sacrificing souls who go forth to serve Uncle Sam in out-of-the-way places. Every citizen of the United States who finds himself in a foreign country invariably hunts up our representative, and expects to make the Consulate his headquarters.

He leaves packages there to be taken care of, uses the official desk for corresponding purposes, helps himself to the stationery and winds up by borrowing stamps to mail his letters—he also expects the Consul to drive him around the city and introduce him to the President. If in need of information he goes there to find it, if hard up he expects assistance, if "dead broke" a passage home, and if the poor worm of an official should sometimes turn feebly on the oppressor, he arouses a storm of indignant protest, sometimes followed by a letter addressed to the authorities at Washington. Such is the wail of this much abused class, but with all its sorrows, dissappointments and keen regrets, its terrors and its tears—there seems no lack of candidates for the uncomfortable position.

CHAPTER XII.

CITY OF GRENADA—HOTEL DE LOS LEONS.

This city, at one time the capitol of the Republic, is about the same size as Leon, and its deadly rival. During the past century many conflicts have resulted from this spirit of jealousy, causing great loss of life and the destruction of millions of dollars worth of property. Of the two towns, Grenada is the most desirable as a place of residence; its situation on the shore of the beautiful Lake Nicaragua, gives it an advantage that Leon can never hope to equal.

Here we stopped at the "Hotel De Los Leons." This very interesting structure is a relic of the old days of the Spanish dominion with high arched entrances provided with huge oak doors, which still hold the bullets they received during the numerous revolutions through which the city has passed. The building was erected by the church in the early days, and was for many years used as a convent; afterwards fitted up for a hotel, and is even more comfortable and inviting than the "Golden Lion" of Leon. Its proprietor, Mr. Downing, is a native of the United States, but having become fascinated with the climate and the beautiful daughter of a wealthy Don, he succumbed to the double attraction and has abandoned his native land to become a citizen of the country.

The house occupies both sides of the plaza from which it takes its name, the "Plazuela De Los Leons," (little plaza of the lions.) The main entrance consists of a massive arch elaborately carved; on the frieze over the doors two lions of conventional pattern regard each other with a stony stare. Both seemed somewhat low-spirited, if the countenance is any indication of mental condition. Both are chained to the wall to prevent escape. Above these chained images, and filling the upper section of the arch, is the graven representation of the arms of Ferdinand the 7th. This portion of the work has suffered much from the ravages of time as well as bullets, the soft sandstone being so badly weather beaten that some of the finer lines are quite obliterated. In a crevice of the rock work a musket ball is sticking, a memento of the days of Walker, who made things very lively here in 1856. The doors, constructed of four inch oak planks securely bolted on to beams of proportionate strength, were splintered by musket balls and torn by cannon shot. Several large ragged holes attested the earnest character of the engagement. These great doors remain precisely as they were left by the insurgents and form one of the most interesting landmarks of the city.

Mr. Downing informed us that he had been offered $2000 for this pair of doors by an enthusiastic relic hunter, but he declared they were worth twice that sum as an advertisement of his house. So it will be seen that, while he had given up his title as a citizen of the chilly north, he still held fast to his early commercial training, the first principle of which is judicious advertising.

The following from the New York Herald for August 17, 1889, shows with what eagerness such old time sovenirs are sought by a certain class of cranks, who possess the means of satisfying their craving for the curious. It also shows the accuracy of the reporter.

"By telegraph to the Herald. Marlborough, N. Y. Two cedar doors over 480 years old have been received by Mead & Taft at Cornwall, from Mexico, to be placed in the residence of Mrs. R. S. Hays, at Millbrook, Dutchess County, N. Y. These doors were taken from one of the old Catholic monasteries which were erected in Mexico directly after the great massacre in the year 1400. Each door is four feet by eight feet in size, four inches thick and they weigh 600 pounds each. The stiles and rails are worked from solid wood and are fastened with wooden nails. There were probably no hinges when the doors were made as they appear to have been hung on pivots. The wood carving is plain and deep and one door bears a fine specimen of the art in the form of a cross of leaves. These relics were purchased by Mrs. Hays during a recent tour through Mexico."

The above appeared in the Sunday Herald and helped to fill space that might have been devoted to legitimate advertising at the rate of $2.00 per line. It's a pity the correspondent omitted to name the price paid for the lumber, it must have been considerable. Doors taken from a Catholic monastery in Mexico, which flourished nearly a century before the discovery of America would naturally be valuable. It is also interesting to learn something of the great massacre that occured ninety-two years before Columbus sailed from Spain on his first western voyage. We would be glad to have fuller particulars, but to know that it occured and that the pious survivors immediately began the erection of this ancient building, is very gratifying. It is also intensely interesting to read about the cross of leaves, which native fervor designed a hundred years in advance of the appearance of that symbol of Christianity in the Western Hemisphere. Taken altogether, there is a considerable amount of information tied up in the dispatch from Marlborough that will be of great value to the historian and antiquarian.

At Leon and Managua, we found the hotel crowded with travelers from all parts of the world, attracted by glowing accounts published by the literary staff of the Maritime Canal Co. Most of these adventurers had entered Nicaragua through the western gate, coming down from California, Mexico, Gautemala and the mining

THE ARTIST'S DREAM OF LIFE IN THE TROPICS. M. O. H.

districts of Honduras. All were pressing eagerly forward to Greytown (San Juan Del Norte,) where they confidently expected to secure employment at almost any rate they might demand. A few had been down to headquarters, and being disappointed, were now retracing their steps, invoking blessings of doubtful import on the heads of the officials of the company.

We spent some time looking over this old town and found much to interest and amuse. The intense pride and egotism of the native born citizen is unparalleled. The majority of these people have never been beyond the limits of the town, apparently, and fully believe Grenada to be the largest, richest and finest city on the globe. A cabman insisted that the population exceeded 200,-000 and pointed with pride to the grass grown towers of La Merced, declaring that its like would not be found in any other city. There were many mementoes of Merry William Walker's brief, but bloody campaign, rows of deserted houses with broken walls and fallen roofs, over which kind nature has thrown a cloak of swaying vines; tall trees have crowded up through the rotten rafters, and bright green lizards flash across the sunlit patches in pursuit of their prey. These were the homes of the aristocrats half a century ago and the fancy iron work of the projecting windows may still be seen covered with a thick coating of rust. Carefully we picked our way through one of these crumbling ruins. The interior was filled with decaying timbers, the dense growth of vegetation overhead caused a darkness akin to night, strange fungus forms covered walls and casement, some of a bright yellow, others as red as blood and still others of a silvery whiteness which glowed with a phoresent light. Under the rubbish we found the old tile floors in perfect condition with here and there a fragment of brass, green with age. Beyond, in the inner court we discovered the ancient basin of a fountain long since silent. The space was filled with trees and shrubbery, so dense the growth that scarcely a ray of sunshine penetrated to the ground. Here were great logs, the remains of trees that had attained their full growth and fallen in their tracks, where they lay covered with moss and lichens. We found a melancholy pleasure in exploring these old time mansions. We could imagine them restored to their early granduer, the tiled floors were relieved by costly rugs, there were tables of oak with massive carved legs, the luxurious divan with its oriental silks, huge uncomfortable chairs of ancient pattern. Roses and oleanders fill the court with beauty and fragrance, the fountain restored, sends up a spray-like jet that cools the air like a breath from the ocean, and falling softly over a bed of shells bordered by ferns, makes drowsy music. The old Don is sitting under the balcony half asleep; a sharp eyed duenna is busily engaged on a piece of elaborate needle work, but not so busily as to overlook the actions of a young lady, who is apparently absorbed in her studies, but who is slyly reading a note which she has skillfully disposed between the pages of her book. A beautiful green parrot, who enjoys the freedom of the yard, repeats slowly "Don

Jose, Don Jose—Don." The young lady rises and taking poll across the inclosure whispers, "naughty poll—how could you"— then she returns to her seat with a ruddy glow on her cheeks that was not there before.

It is evening, the full moon sheds a silvery radiance over the street, a bright-eyed senoita stands at the barred window, she is gazing dreamily on this beautiful scene, still there is an anxious look in her dark eyes. Here and there lights are seen among the deep shadows of the trees. Just across the way a traveling musician is playing some old Spanish airs, soon a crowd gathers about him, then a figure closely muffled separates itself from the throng, approaches the window softly, silently—it stops before the iron grating; anxious eyes are smiling now, there is a swift pressure of hands, a touching of lips between those cruel bars, a whispered consultation, a letter passed in; a light appears—Don Jose glides into the shadow; the Duenna finds only a young lady gazing dreamily on the moonlit street.

The large airy rooms of the hotel open upon a wide balcony overlooking the central court with its masses of flowers and shimmering fountains; here you may sit and smoke, enjoying the present or speculating on the future, your ears filled the while with the music of singing birds and the murmur of falling water—but a traveler cannot always tarry in one place, no matter how pleasant the surroundings, so one morning we had our baggage placed on board a pretty little steamer that was being loaded for Castillo, a village on the San Juan River situated about midway between Fort San Carlos and Greytown. We had the pleasure of seeing the hold stowed with connical shells, packages of powder and several hundred stands of small arms, for at that time the air was full of rumors of war. Costi Rica was watching every movement of her more powerful neighbor with jealous eyes, while it was openly charged that Bogran's recent visit to Gautemala was for the purpose of entering into an alliance by which the combined forces of that country and Honduras would be hurled against Nicaragua, therefore, all this military activity.

Lake Nicaragua is one of the most beautiful sheets of water in the world, deep, transparent, sparkling. Its shore scenery, with its ever-changing features cannot be excelled. Now we pass high rocky precipices overrun with vines, and crowned with trees that hang their long branches far over the water. Now the forest comes down to the very edge of the lake and again there will be found wide, bright green glades with here and there a clump of live oaks, their rich, dark foliage contrasting finely with the lighter tints of the grass. Occasionally we passed the hut of some lonely fishermen almost hidden among the bananas, which furnish his living, while he drags the lake for the city market.

This lake, has an extreme length of about 90 miles, and is nearly 45 miles across at its widest point. It takes its name from the Cacique Nicaro, a chief of some importance. He was the head of a numerous tribe of Indians, who resided on the banks in the neighborhood of the present town of Rivas, enjoying peace and plenty, until one unhappy day an old Spanish freebooter named Gil Gonzalez, discovered their retreat and gave them the choice of accepting the christian faith or being shot. They weakly accepted the first option and quietly went into slavery of the most degrading character. Such was the reward awaiting the converts of these evangelistic robbers of the sixteenth century. Could this old Cacique have forseen the consequences of the step he took that day he would have accepted the last alternative and died like a man, both he and his tribe, as it was, they lay down their arms and were baptized in the beautiful lake to the number of several thousand, and in reporting the occurance to the king, old Gil spoke of this lake as "Nicaro's Agua," which with slight modification, it retains to this day.

We stopped at Rivas long enough to take on a number of cattle, which were driven out over the long, narrow bridge that connects the landing with the shore about an eighth of a mile away; many women also came out to meet the boat, bringing curios, such as cocoanut shells, ebonized, polished and engraved in elaborate and fantastic patterns. They also carried fruits, eggs and sweet breads. The cattle were quickly loaded by means of the steam crane. A strong rope was thrown over their long, spreading horns. The engine started, in a moment the animal found himself swinging between heaven and earth, the next he was dropped uncermoniously on the lower deck, where they were closely tied to the rail to bellow and complain during the remainder of the voyage.

Stopped again at San Carlos to discharge those shells and

rifles. While this was going on, we amused ourselves shooting at some alligators who seemed to enjoy the sport, at least they continued to swim around and smile, which is an indication of amusement.

From San Carlos we have a fine view of the mountains of Costi Rica, their bold outlines rising far above the clouds. At the fort, everything was bustle and confusion. A few dozen soldiers under the command of a French army officer, were busily engaged in digging ditches, throwing up enbankments, constructing magazines, mounting some ancient field pieces, that promise to be more destructive to the garrison than the enemy.

MAKING TORTILLOS.

This fort is situated at the head of the San Juan River, which supplied by this magnificent reservoir, begins its course full fledged and navigable for large boats from its very source to where it enters the harbor at San Juan Del Norte, or Greytown, with the exception of a distance of about one-fourth of a mile at Castillo, where the rapids occur.

Having finished discharging her cargo of explosives and taken on a few more victims who had drifted thus far hoping to find immediate employment on the canal, the pilot turned the prow of the little steamer into the river and we were soon floating between banks beautifully diversified by forest and glade with here and there a patch of cultivated ground, though the open land seemed mostly devoted to grazing purposes. We passed some fields of maze, others of rice, a few orange trees, a few small banana plantations, but for more than one hundred miles the shores were lined by an almost impenetrable jungle.

Thus floating gently along, amid scenery of the most pleasing character, we arrived at the village of Castillo, which consists principally of one street strung along on a little shelf lying between the river and a series of high bluffs, on one of which we could trace the dark outline of the fort, from which the place takes its name. This fortification is splendidly situated, commanding as it does, the river and all approaches to the town. This is the fort that so discouraged Lord Nelson that he gave up the idea of capturing it and returned home, at least a year older, if not sadder and wiser.

From San Carlos we had been following the course of the much talked of canal that was to "change the tide of commerce," and thus affect, in a measure, the "destiny of all civilized nations." We strained our eyes and ears for some sign of the great work that we were led to suppose was being carried rapidly forward, but, both eye and ear were alike disappointed. There was neither sight nor sound to indicate that we were in the midst of the "greatest enterprise of modern times." The picturesque shores were silent and deserted with the exception of a few miserable huts occupied by herdsmen and their families. Our fellow passengers, some of whom had come thousands of miles expecting to find a ready demand for their labor or talents, gazed on this scene of desolation with ever-increasing disgust. They saw no beauty in the silent forest with its dense shadows and wonderful array of vines and creepers that over run the tallest trees, the broken cliff or open glade were alike uninteresting. Like the disappointed gold seekers of Honduras, they were blind and deaf to everything but the fact that they had come on a fool's errand and must return with a fool's reward.

The transfer of baggage and freight occupied two days, so we had plenty of time to explore the village and visit the fort, which we were invited to do by the Commandante, who took great pride in showing us over this ancient fortification, which had successfully stood out for months against the great Nelson.

Castillo is a miserable little village having no interest for the traveler aside from the ancient fort and the fact that this is the point selected for the construction of a dam and lock, the former sixty-five feet in height by 1500 feet in length, which will submerge the town and raise the level of the river to that of the lake which forms its source, so that the ship having once attained this elevation will meet with no further obstruction until it arrives within three miles of the Pacific, where it will begin its descent to the sea by a rapid series of steps, dropping down 110 feet to the harbor of Brito or San Juan Del Sur through three locks known as No. 4, 5, and 6. As a matter of course this improvement will destroy the present town and as the officials declared that work would begin immediately on the arrival of men and machinery, which were then actually on their way from New York, (their departure from that port had been cabled,) the residents exhibited no alarm and we found the people could not be induced to regard the scheme in a serious light. Old men had witnessed the rise and fall of canal booms at periods more or less regular from their earliest recollections, besides they had an accumulated stock of legends of the same sort inherited from their fathers and grand-fathers.

We met some engineers at this point, who were looking over the ground and constructing the dam on paper. It looked very pretty and realistic. A very large ship was being raised and interested passengers were leaning on the rail watching proceedings. It was an odd spectacle to see this huge Atlantic liner maneuvering in the woods with cocoanut trees bending over and sweeping the deck. I think the picture showed some of the passengers picking the nuts as they passed. The author of this design was more than a draughtsman, more than an artist, more than a poet—he was a prophet, whose sharp vision found no difficulty in penetrating the mists that hang over the horizon of the future. He had even attired the passengers of this phantom ship with garments undreamed of by the most farseeing leader of fashion. All this was to be accomplished by the summer of 1894—at the very farthest 1895!

While here we witnessed the celebration of St. Jeromes Day. Just what St. Jerome did to deserve such noisy honors, we could not learn. That he flourished 1600 years ago and was a diligent student and traveler, as well as a writer of religious literature, was perhaps excuse enough for the loud demonstration tendered his waxen image, which was covered with flowers and carried the length of the street, proceeded by a dozen masked men, each of whom was armed with a wooden sword with which they engaged in playful combat, the main object being to knock off each others hats or break the opponents weapon, either event being followed by the enthusiastic applause of the crowd. Following the figure came a procession attired in all manner of outlandish costumes, some blowing horns, others discharging rockets. The Cabildo and principal stores were decorated with palms and flowers, and all business suspended, except that of the vender of aguardiente and similar fiery fluids—consequently many of the swordsmen were using thir sticks very earnestly indeed before the day was over, and heads instead of hats were the objects of attack. Whenever one was "knocked out" the officers carried the hero to the Cabildo, where he was rubbed back to life or taken away by his friends.

The transfer of goods having been completed at last, we found ourselves on board a very ancient stern wheeler, that had been worn out as a frieghter on the lower Missisippi a generation since, but which was considered quite equal to the demands of the San Juan.

The lower deck was crowded with cattle, and the upper floors were none to clean, however, the discomforts of the boat were forgotten in the contemplation of the scenery of this remarkable river, rivaling that of the Amazon in the richness and variety of its vegetation, while the broad smoothly flowing stream reflected every leaf with the accuracy of a mirror—the forest dense as a wall came down to the water's edge—masses of flowering vines swayed in the breeze, adding the charm of color—birds of brilliant plumage made frequent excursions from shore to shore—there were parrots, green, scarlet and golden, but the most beautiful bird was the white Heron, which we noted at times, standing, sentinel-like, where the mouth of a stream formed a shallow bay overhung with foliage—strange sounds, too, came from behind these green walls—denizens of the forest, contesting for some choice prize—maybe.

Refering to my note book I find we arrived at Greytown about 11 P. M. but did not go on shore until morning—when we registered at the "Hotel Victoria" kept by Mrs. Kimball, an English lady, who doubtless thinks to honor her sovereign by thus borrowing her title.

As usual, we found the town filled with strangers waiting for the canal. Every boat bought new adventurers. Some had been on the ground over a year, expecting to see active operations at any time, many were suffering from fever.

The town consists of two long streets, lined with frame houses thatched with palm leaves. The land is perfectly level. On every side extend bayous lined with mangrove swamps, ripe with malaria and deadly fevers, not to mention the clouds of mosquitoes and sand flies. A vertical sun fairly scorches the earth

MOMOTOMBO.

between showers, which occur almost daily during the dry months and day and night the rest of the year.

The only pleasant feature of the place is the great variety of tropical fruits that abound, and which attain here their greatest perfection. Every garden is an orchard filled with orange, cocoanut and bread fruit trees. The square or plaza, is lined with mangos, whose dense foliage make a most grateful shade—when the sun shines. Here we buy twelve oranges for five cents, equal to Florida's best, bananas for the picking. The population consists largely of Jamaica negroes, with a sprinkling of Caribs, the whites being in the minority.

Not many persons survive through a half century in this climate, but one such we found who had witnessed the bombardment which occured in the early fifties; having some curiosity to learn why an American captain should be so foolish as to waste good powder and shot on such miserable huts as those about us, we sought this ancient man, whose long, white beard and deeply furrowed cheeks, told of years of suffering and innumerable encounters with the fevers that carry away about nine-tenths of the inhabtants who have the temerity to remain among these pestilential wilds.

"Well" said he, "let me see, it's been a good while ago, and though I remember the day, with the excitement and terror that all but paralyzed the poor Indians and Negros, who would not have been more frightened if told that the end of the world was at hand, yet I cannot at this late hour give any accurate account of the causes leading thereto. The wretched inhabitants fled in every direction seeking safety in the vast swamps, where they crouched like hunted beasts, during the hours of that shameful and inexcusable canonade. Of course, every one now acknowledges that the Americans where wholly at fault, but I have never learned that any adequate remuneration was made for the property destroyed or any apology offered for the insult to a sister republic, albeit a very weak and defenceless one.

As near as I can remember the circumstances, they were about like this:—The captain of an American steamer, one of a line running between this port and New York, being ashore one day—think it was in May, had been drinking a little more than a prudent captain should, meeting a negro on the street he began to abuse him and when the fellow resented the attack the captain drew his revolver and shot him down. There was no excuse whatever for the outrage. It was a deliberate, cold-blooded murder. Of course, the officials were soon notified, and the Alcalde and deputies started in pursuit of the murderer, who being unable to escape to his vessel, sought refuge under the flag of the American Consulate. Of course the place was soon surrounded by a crowd of angry, excited negroes, who loudly demanded his surrender, but the American Minister, Borland, I think was his name, refused to give up the fugitive, thereupon the mob became more boisterous. Some cried, 'Burn the office,' 'Pull down the flag,' 'Hang them both.' Meanwhile some shots were actually fired at the ensign and, had it not been for the Alcalde the mob would have had their will. As it was, a number of missles were thrown, one of which struck Mr. Boland, causing an ugly, though not dangerous wound. Meanwhile word had reached an American vessel that was lying in the harbor and a boat was sent under a strong guard to take off the guilty captain, which having been accomplished, fifty thoroughly armed men were left to protect the property of the transit company. Of course, the incident was promptly reported at Washington in such a light that the captain was made to appear a martyr, and an armed sloop was at once dispatched to the scene, which arriving before the town, the commander immediately informed the authorities that he would bombard the place within a few hours. Then there was weeping and wailing. Women ran up and down the streets screaming, some with their armed filled with trinkets hastily gathered up, others carrying helpless babies, whose piteous cries added to the confusion. The men were even more excited, and though scared half to death, the desire to save their scanty hoards rose above the dangers of the hour and while some ran back and forth wringing their hands in helpless agony, the majority were bending under loads of furniture, bedding, dishes, clocks and mirrors. Still others were hurriedly burrying their jewelry and plate in all sorts of odd corners, some of which have never been located to this day.

One old white-haired darkey was seen struggling with an enormous clock of ancient pattern. It was fully a foot taller that its owner. The heavy weights rolled from side to side while the striking apparatus, dislocated by such rough usage, kept up a sonorous protest, solemnly telling of the hours regardless of time and place. However, it proved too much for the old fellow, who, after dragging it a hundred yards or so, was forced to abandon it. As the hour of doom approached, the streets became almost deserted, and when the first shot was fired the only response it aroused was the dismal howls sent up by a band of stray dogs, who crowded together as though for mutual protection.

Of course, no great damage resulted from the bombardment of a town of straw huts, and after the captain had knocked a few of the flimsey structures to pieces and destroyed a few more by the torch, he withdrew, but it was a long time before the darkies recovered from their fright and the very mention of an American was enough to cause a panic." But this was when we were a young and foolish nation—such hot haste to avenge the wrongs, real or fancied of American citizens in these days would be considered quite out of place—undiplomatic—the conservative element of our dear country would be shocked beyond measure, at the bare suggestion of sending a war vessel to enforce the rights of American citizens which are being daily outraged by the Spanish barbarians in the

CAMP SAN FRANCISCO, SAN JUAN RIVER.

Island of Cuba—as witness the call of Gen. Lee recently issued in behalf of the murdered Dr. Ruiz—and dozens of other cases equally aggravating. *

The New York steamer "Hondo" having arrived, we took passage for Belize, and ten days later found ourselves once more before the capitol of the little British Colony where our wanderings began a few months earlier. The harbor was calm and beautiful and the view from the steamer's deck seemed even more charming than on our first visit. A slight haze hung over the distant coxcomb mountains, several large sailing vessels and the usual crowd

---

* Written before the desecration of war—a course which ought in justice to ourselves, and in the name of humanity been entered upon twenty years earlier, that it was not, is sufficient evidence of the peaceful character of the great American nation.

of smaller water crafts lay rocking in the bay, among which the Carib Dory was as ever conspicuous.

The custom house officer having examined our various trunks and valises and finding nothing contraband, we were allowed to send them ashore, where we followed shortly and were soon comfortably established at the "Union Hotel." Naturally our first thoughts were of Mr. Horn and the millions which he came to rescue from the grasping sands of Turneff Island. I thought he would need some help to handle such a large amount of heavy metal and so proposed to offer my services. I therefore, made inquiry immediately to learn where he was stopping so that I might hasten to congratulate him upon the successful completion of his labors and place my knowledge of finance at his disposal—for a considertion. Judge my sorrow and disappointment when I learned that the enterprise had been abandoned months before. The story is soon told. Mr. Horn and his companion, were kept waiting nearly six weeks before they received official sanction to begin the search. Each day of delay caused an increase of anxiety, as he imagined the governor was lending his influence to another party who were working day and night to get in ahead and thus deprive him of the opportunity of his life. The disappointment thus incurred from week to week, so told upon his health that when he finally came into possession of the longed for document, he was scarcely able to undertake the work. However, he hired a number of men and tools, and moved over to the scene of action. They had just begun operations under the most favorable auspices when a heavy storm arose, during which implements, boats and supplies were mostly swept away by the waves and Mr. Horn was drowned by the capsizing of his dory. His partner, whose faith had never been strong, now abandoned the project and returned to the States. Thus ended another chapter in the long history of disasters that has followed the treasure hunter from time immemorial, but with all these evidences of the utter folly of seeking imaginary wealth, where horse sense would teach that the chances of success are less than one in a million, the dealers in divining rods continue to flourish and the clairvoyant still points outs pots of gold for any fool who has an ordinary silver dollar to exchange for such information, and when they fail to find the treasure the attribute it to ill luck or some "evil influence," and lock the secret of their folly in their hearts instead of falling on their deceivers and reducing them to fine powder. We wished to return via New Orleans, but soon learned that, although the Central American coast is the most healthful of any in the world, the foolish officers composing the board of health of the Crescent City, refused to receive passengers from this and neighboring ports. Galveston and Mobile were also quarantined against us, and the only avenue to escape was to take passage for New York or Norfolk, Va. While waiting for a vessel, we spent our time calling on old friends. Among others, we ran across an Englishman whom we had met in the mountains of Santa Barbara, about three months previous. He was then on his way to Belize. His home was at Ségautápeca, an Indian Peublo, which happened to be on our route. When he learned that we would pass through the place, he insisted that we should stop at his house. He said that he had been a resident of Honduras over thirty years. He came to the country in 1859, expecting to make a fortune in a few months in the mines, but soon found he was putting more gold into the earth than he was getting out, and having recorded a solemn vow to the effect that he would never return to England until he could take a fortune with him, he began looking around for some more profitable field of labor, the longed-for opening did not appear, and after drifting from place to place, experimenting with fruits, coffee and nutmegs, making a little one season only to loose it the next, he was surprised to find ten years had slipped away and the fortune still as far in the distance as when he first landed, but his determination to make a "stake" before returning to his native land was still unbroken. Pondering on the situation one day, he conceived the brilliant idea of marrying the daughter of a wealthy Don, whose acquaintance he had made in one of his trips through the department of Santa Barbara, the old chap was the owner of several square miles of fine grazing lands, sprinkled over with some three thousand head of lean stock, in fact he was regarded as a cattle king in his day, but of all his possessions, Senorita Marie, his only daughter, was by far the most precious, and it was no wonder that the young Englishman should fall before the glances of those eyes that had already proved fatal to a dozen or more native suitors. At the time we speak of, the old ranchman was preparing for his annual pilgrimage to the city of Guatemala, the metropolis of Central America, and the great cattle market for a wide stretch of country.

Every year the Don with a half dozen herdsmen would make this trip driving their long horned cattle over the mountains, covering about two leagues a day on an average. This was the Don's one distraction; and was looked forward to for weeks. A month was usually spent on the road and a week at the gay capitol. It was during this time that our friend, taking advantage of the hospitality that opens every door to the stranger, made his home with the family of the absent lord, where his social talents soon captured every heart; the Don was growing old. The ever increasing business demanded a man of affairs to oversee the Hacienda, keep

CASTILLO, NICARAGUA.

accounts and act as general manager. Who could be better fitted for such a position than the Englishman. The place was offered at a salary that was quite satisfactory. Six months latter, the beautiful Marie was included in the contract, and the marriage duly solemnized in the village church amid great rejoicing, and this was how it came to pass that plain Bill Barlow became a Senor Don, and the owner of more acres than he could count, for he had not only kept the family estate intact but had added to it by degrees, until his cattle now range for miles over mountain and plain. All this and much more, he related as we sat and smoked under the shade of the long gallaries of the Union Hotel. Among other yarns he related was the true history of the word "Gringo," now universally applied to English and American travelers or residents, but especially applicable to those vagrant characters, who roam from place to place without any apparent business such as newspaper correspondents, artists, musicians and the like good-for-nothing tramps. The origin of this expressive phrase, Don William assured us, might be traced back to the early sixties—probably sixty-one.

That year a party of young Scotch students made a tour of the country in the guise of minstrels. They had a royal good time, singing the songs of Auld Lang Syne, and making love to the pretty daughters of the unsophisticated farmers who felt themselves highly honored by the attention of the gay foreigners, whose words they could not understand, but whose sentiments needed no interpreter, and many a girl of that day remembers the moonlit walks, the music, and the vows so solemnly pledged under the spreading boughs of the giant ceiba tree, which threw its black shadows across the path just at the proper time and place!

The leading song by which this party of happy roustabouts became known, was that charming ditty by Burns, which so accurately reflected the minds of the singers, "Green grow the rashes O," while the natives could not understand a word of the language, they were entranced by its melody, and the first two words merged into one with a slight modification, became typical of foreigners in general and English in particular.

So strong the impression made by this simple jingle, that the first verses may still be heard repeated by the native singers to whom the words remain a mystery.

> "Green grow the rashes O,
> Green grow the rashes O,
> The sweetest hours that e'er I spend,
> Are spent among the lasso O."
>
> There's naught but care on every hand,
> In every hour that passes O,
> What signifies the life of man,
> And 'twere not for the lasses O?"

This is Don William's version—it may be true—or it may have been an innocent invention of Mr. Barlow's to help pass away the time, or secure undying fame by getting his name in this book.

A week later the writer stepped on the wharf at Norfolk, in a howling blizzard of snow—and the scenes and incidents herein described, became a memory of the past—a dream from which all that was disagreeable speedily faded. Fleas, ants, scorpions, tarantulas and centipedes were forgotten—only the glorious sky with its never ending procession of days filled with golden sunlight were recalled, and sometimes during the winter that followed he would imagine that he could detect the odor of orange blossoms when the wind blew softly from the south, as it sometimes does in February; or some distant sound at twilight would awaken the memories of the tuneful guitar and the sweet but pathetic Spanish songs, and moonlit streets of Leon and Grenada.

www.ingramcontent.com/pod-product-compliance
Lightning Source LLC
Chambersburg PA
CBHW031832230426
43669CB00009B/1321